FIFTEEN YEARS & 14 CHAPTERS

THE LOSS OF MY SON IN THREE WAYS

NATALIE WATSON

Copyright © 2019 Natalie Watson

ISBN 978-1-9991021-0-4

DEDICATION

MY NAME IS Natalie Watson, I was born and raised in St Vincent and the Grenadines. I am a mother of four beautiful children ages 7, 13, 15 and 19.

This book is dedicated to my late son Noah Matthew Watson. Noah was born on August 13th, 2003 in the city of Toronto and died at the age of fourteen when he passed away on May 30th, 2018, in the city of Welland. Noah lived each and everyday to the fullest, living each and everyday as if it were the last day.

This book is written in remembrance and in honour for my son Noah, a sweet sixteen birthday gift, the gift of his story written and immortalized. Through this book his memory will live on and he will never be forgotten.

If Noah were alive with us, he would be able to tell his own story and his own truth. The stories captured in this book are all true events that took place while Noah was here with us in the physical sense.

My son Noah had a bright personality that lit up

every room he entered. Noah was loved by his family and cared for by many. He was that kid that loved a challenge and would always test the status quo; he was funny, intelligent and full of charisma. Noah enjoyed playing many different sports, with basketball and football being his favourites. Noah always used to say that when he grew up, he wanted to become a professional basketball player in the NBA or an architect working within the construction field like his uncle. He always had big dreams and set goals for himself.

Noah loved and appreciate family functions, he enjoyed family dinner with some good soul food cooking. His favourite time of the year was Thanksgiving and Christmas holidays. Christmas, he particularly enjoyed the most. Shopping and decorating were two activities he was always eager to join in on!

Noah was loved and cared for by his family and friends, he was a real people-person who constantly put himself last amongst his friends. He stood up for others to stop bullying even when he was unsure of the outcome.

Noah will forever be in our hearts, we will never forget him even as the days, months and years pass us by. We will cherish all the good memories; and everything we do, we do it from within our hearts and with purpose and love as we remember him daily.

We love and appreciate all of you Noah Matthew Watson. I wish we could have had more time together and I pray for our Father, God, to keep you within His kingdom. Until our hearts meet and reunites us again, sleep in peace my son.

CONTENTS

Chapter One | 1
A smile to remember from my kids just as they are leaving for school.

Chapter Two | 7
Rewind to 14 years Earlier…The birth of my baby boy Noah Matthew Watson, all the joys of motherhood and Noah's 1st birthday and baptism ceremony.

Chapter Three | 17
Here's to a new beginning moving away from a busy city to a quiet suburban neighbourhood and a difficult decision I had to make to for Noah's and his sisters.

Chapter Four | 29
Noah transitions into his new home at his father's residence, A turning point in my life and in Noah's.

Chapter Five | 37
Having to be persistent while everything changes within a blink of an eye. From a temporary to a permanent home setting, dealing with custody access and the day to day challenges of life.

Chapter Six | 53
Failure, Family and Faith. Dealing with failure from family, failure from the system and almost losing faith during the midst of it all.

Chapter Seven | 65
Out with the old and in with the new. A start of a new beginning. Moving to a new region and Noah moving back home permanently.

Chapter Eight | 73
Getting settled and comfortable in a new environment, adapting to changing things around for the positive..

Chapter Nine | 81
High school junior year - Noah overcame challenges and obstacles throughout his first and second semester. Managing Suspensions and taking responsibility of his actions..

Chapter Ten | 91
My worry as a parent when my teenage child does not return home from school.

Chapter Eleven | 103
Continuation of Chapter One - Fast forward to 15 years later.

Chapter Twelve | 111
The search for Noah within the community by family, friends and strangers turns out to be my family's worst nightmare.

Chapter Thirteen | 125
Healing from being broken hearted, in everyway. I learnt that the only person you can rely on is God and yourself.

Chapter Fourteen | 137
Purpose driven, new relationship and a spiritual connection with Noah, overcoming obstacles that held me back.

Chapter Fifteen | 149
Letters, Messages And Poems To Noah

Final Thoughts | 159

ABOUT THE AUTHOR

NATALIE WATSON was born and raised in St. Vincent and the Grenadines. She's a nurturing mother of four children and a wife. Natalie considers herself a motivator and an inspiration to many. While healing the loss of her son she has found comfort through journal entries, which has turned into writing her first book. Natalie understands and embraces the power of having a positive mindset.

CHAPTER ONE

*A smile to remember from my kids
as they leave for school.*

Tuesday May 29th, 2018

IT WAS TUESDAY May 29th, 2018, the day was bright and sunny, and I was awoken by the sun beaming through my curtains at 6:30 AM. I remember vividly, that the sun was as bright as it was in the middle of summer. I got out of bed to start the usual morning with my children, I went into my bathroom to brush my teeth, and wash my face. I left my room and went into the hallway, where I could see my kids were all up and getting ready for school. I can still hear running water from their bathroom and the shower flowing. I can hear footsteps around the house. Footsteps going from room to room upstairs and downstairs and upstairs again. The sound of doors opening and closing as four children, with happy and cheerful voices, get ready for school. I thought to myself today is a going to be a good day for everyone. Wearing my white robe, without a string to tie it together, I headed downstairs as usual, to make lunch for my two younger children and get breakfast started before they all make their way downstairs. My two older children usually make their own lunches, or they will purchase it from the school cafeteria, it depends on the day and how they are feeling. Noah is my only son; he is 14 years old and my older daughter who is 18 years old were already downstairs in the kitchen area. I checked Noah's attire and gave him an extra stare, thinking that he really looked fresh in his school uniform of a white golf shirt and grey dress pants. It had taken me a lot of Shout, bleach and other stain removers to get the stains and the dirt out over the weekend, and I was happy to have it looking as clean and bright the way it did. I can see both of my two older children in the kitchen moving around appearing rushed as if they were going to miss their school bus that morning. Praying and hoping, I thought to myself: "they better not miss the school bus today!" That morning I had to be at work for 8.30am, and it was not the day for them to miss their bus; today was not the day. I asked Noah if he was going to eat? He replied: "I don't feel like eating," as he went into the fridge and reached for the carton of iced tea. He had a glass in his hands, as he turned around to pour some into the glass before drinking the full glass. On this morning Noah was in a great mood, he had a very happy spirit and he was very cheerful before coming downstairs. I can see his smiles, I can hear his tone of voice as he speaks to his youngest sister who had just walked into the kitchen area after getting ready for school. It was almost time for Noah and his older sister to leave the house to make it for the school bus. The bus stop was just one street over from where we lived. Before heading to the front door Noah finishes what was in his glass and places his glass on the countertop.

Noah was very eager and happy that morning to be back at school after being on a 10-day suspension. "Have an excellent day at school!" Noah says to his younger sister." "Have a great day at work, Mama!" I looked at Noah all I can see is a big bright smile on his face. I looked back at him with an echoing smile and said: "Thank you Noah! You have a good day too! Its your first day back at school."

Noah and his older sister left shortly after he uttered those words to me. As they headed towards the front door to put their shoes on, I watched them both leave, one after the other.

Noah was last to leave as usual, he would always get an extra look at himself in the powder room mirror before heading out.

I watch him put on his black pair of school shoes and take his blue and black Adidas back-pack and head off out the door. As Noah leaves through the front door and closes, it I continue to watch him until, from where I was standing in the kitchen, his reflection from the glass wasn't visible any longer. At this point my two younger children, both daughters, along with my husband, were now in the kitchen having breakfast. Each of them sitting at one of the three red barstools in the kitchen.

I had packed my lunch from the night before, I grabbed it from the fridge and gathered up my personal belongings: my phone, keys and water bottle.

Shortly after, my two younger daughters finished up in the kitchen and made their way to the front foyer area before setting out to catch their school bus also.

Then it was my turn to leave the house and head to work as they were leaving. As I walked towards the front door, I looked at my younger two kids and told both to have a great day at school. I can remember how everyone seemed to be in a good happy space as well that morning. Not that its unusual for them to be in a happy place; but I appreciated those mornings when all four kids would wake up for school in good moods. It made it easier to get them out on time. Three girls and one boy can be a bit of a challenge. There was never a dull moment in the house, especially when it came to using the bathroom, sometimes one would be taking a shower, while another would be on the toilet and another would be using the sink brushing teeth or combing hair, while Noah is knocking the door reminding them that he also needs to still do his things! There was never a dull moment in our house like I said. Music blasting from the basement, the television playing loud movies. In the middle of all of this I will be in the kitchen preparing meals. Let's not forget the laundry also. To describe it best my house was "lit." Noah will often use that word whenever something was fun for him or when he's at his peak. Driving to work

I was also in a great mood as well. My kids had started off the morning in good spirits. I was filling in that day for my co-worker, working Monday to Friday 8:30-4:30. The best shift ever! As I went about my day, I remember it being busy at work I was in and out of the office and I thought how hot it was and thought it was the perfect day to go to the beach or pool.

It was now 2:55pm I thought to myself that my older daughter and Noah would be home off the school bus now and my younger two daughters, shortly after would be home as well. I couldn't wait to go home and spend time with my kids that day. They were all so happy. I had planned on doing something special that day, perhaps going out for ice cream right after dinner. It was 4:30pm the end of my workday. My husband had driven me into work that morning. We were sharing cars that week, as one month previously I had got into a car accident and my car was written off. I was in the process of looking for another vehicle after returning a rental that I had had for a month. In the meantime, my husband would drop me off and pick me up daily depending on his work schedule. That same evening my husband was picking me up from work after having to dropped me off that morning. On our way home, he had told me Noah did not return home after school was finished. Automatically we both though he had gone to the local YMCA to play a game of basketball with his friends. The day was hot in the late evening and the temperature outside were feeling like a 35 degree day, as we got closer to the house I can see a lot of kids out enjoying the beautiful sunshine around the canal banks and along the side walk on bikes and scooters, skateboarders were out in the skate park as well, skating from left to right in the newly build skate park. I was looking out the window feeling pleased with how my day went, it was the first hot day we had since the season started.

CHAPTER TWO

Rewind to 14 years Earlier…
The birth of my baby boy Noah Matthew
Watson, all the joys of motherhood, Noah's
1st birthday and baptism ceremony.

August 13th, 2003

I WAS ONLY 23 years of age when I conceived Noah.

I know what you might be thinking two kids at 23 years of age. Was I out of my mind? At this point in my life I had already left my mother's house and was living on my own, but not for too long. I returned home to live with my mother when things weren't going the greatest for me. With little college education and limited work experience I found it very difficult to take care of myself and two children both under the age of five. One of the happiest days of my life was finding out that I was pregnant with my second child. When I found out I was pregnant I prayed that God would bless me with a boy. With my first born I was blessed with a girl and now I hoped to be blessed with having a baby boy. Even though I was a young mother I enjoyed being pregnant. The whole process brought me great joy, knowing that I will have someone who will look up at me was just beyond wonderful. On August 13th, 2003 I was ready to bring my baby boy into the world. Carrying him for nine months, watching my stomach grow as he got bigger was one of the best feelings I've had.

This pregnancy was different. It wasn't your ideal perfect setting, I didn't plan on having another baby when I got pregnant and my life wasn't set up how I imagined it would be at the time; however I was prepared to bring my baby into the world no matter the odds. Through out my pregnancy, I sensed my baby's warmth in my uterus, could feel him moving around as he grew. With every kick and movement, I knew he was a healthy, happy growing baby boy even before I brought him into the world.

During my pregnancy, when I was about five months along, we traveled to Trinidad and Tobago, I could feel that my baby boy loved it when I visited the beach there or when I was close to the lake. I would lie in the sand and listen to the water as the waves would come up. I can recall going into the water it was always a calm feeling being present and at one with nature.

I knew my baby was going to come into a world filled

with love around him. I was ready to move to another country during those times to make the best life for him and to remain in love. As a mother who had already given birth to my first born, I knew what to prepare for and what to expect when experiencing labour. My bags were packed in advance, and his room was already set up for him at my mother's house in her basement where I stayed. The only thing I was waiting for was his arrival.

During the last thirty days I was restless and couldn't sleep much at nights, most expectant mothers can attest to this, lack of sleep, dark circles under your eyes and the feeling of the weight that sits on your thighs whether you're walking sitting or just simply standing is unbearable at this point.

At the doctor's office with my regular checkups consisted of ultrasounds and examinations, I was told my baby was going to be a big boy. For my first pregnancy I wanted to wait and be surprised, but this time I didn't want any surprises. I can recall laying there as the cold gel hits my lower abdominal area, looking at the screen and listening to his heart beat, at first it was hard to figure out from the position he was in, but he eventually moved around enough and it was clear as day light to determine if it was going to be a boy or a girl. Leaving the doctor's office with my ultrasound photos I was so happy when I received the news, I was smiling on the inside as well on the outside there's nothing anyone could have done or say to me at the time to take that feeling or memory away. I experienced what it feels like to be on cloud nine. Eventually the time approached quicker than I anticipated. It felt like I was waiting for an eternity and then the feeling of a sudden rush in the end.

I recall experiencing mild pain that morning when I woke up but didn't think anything of it. I went about my regular day taking it easy, but by the late evening the pain increased more.

I went into labour, I could feel the contractions as the time went by, the pain was familiar, like the pain I had had with my first born, except the only difference was that it was more intense to bear. I had moved into my mothers house a few months back, this was to make things easier for myself and my children. I had to make some sacrifices in order to move ahead, it felt like 10 steps backwards at the time, the only reason I felt that way was because I never had had a strong relationship with my mother, so it felt as though I was setting myself up for a disaster.

My contractions were getting closer and the pain increased as the minutes passed. I went to the hospital and was sent home because I wasn't dilated enough, then my water broke. I went back to the hospital and I was determined that I was not going home, in the end they decided to keep me. It was at North Finch General Hospital where I gave birth to my precious baby boy. He was given the name "Noah Matthew Joseph," as his three names, and was named after three prophets in the Bible. I wish I could say that I was involved with such strong names, but I will not take the credit from my significant other at that time. He felt that it was important for a boy child to have a strong name. He always said and believed that Noah would be a leader, both as a child and when he was grown. Boy was he right. This was another one of the happiest moments of my life. The excitement of having my second child and an only son was a feeling that I couldn't explain. When he was born, he had the cutest baby face. He was so precious and pure. His tiny little body only weighing 7lbs 8oz cuddled up in my arms was also one of the best experiences I've also had. Noah being the baby brother to his sister was also one of the happiest days for her as well. She was so excited and happy when she became an older sister. She was three years old at the time when he was born.

Just like every new mom whether you're having your first child or fourth, its different each time. Every child is different in their own way. I had to get used to the late nights with bottle feeding and the changing of diapers all over again. This time around though, it was easier and more familiar. I felt like an expert! I was up at times before Noah would wake up, we had a routine. Noah was the type of baby that was very spoiled in a good way, he always received lots of attention from family members and very close friends. With him being the only baby in my mother's house at that time he never lacked being held by someone or played with and he received lots of hugs and kisses as a baby.

Noah enjoyed a good bottle of formula or cornmeal or oatmeal porridge from a young age. Whenever he was finishing having his bottles or there wasn't enough porridge in the bottle he would always cry and pout for more. As the months went by, I watched him grow into a happy and beautiful baby, who would always smile and was ready to play. The energy Noah had was compared to having twin babies. Non-stop energy daily, he was always in a happy place. Noah and his older sister bonded very well, wherever his sister was, you could guarantee that Noah was right behind her. Pulling or tugging away at her clothing. They enjoyed playing with one another, but there were times when his older sister wasn't in the mood for him knocking over her toys or taking her favourite doll and hiding them somewhere that no one will know or having his way with it on the floor pretending it was his toy truck or a robot! They developed and had a bond like no other, one that was inseparable.

Everyone loved and adored Noah, and Noah would somehow always have a special place in their hearts after meeting him, even if it was only for a short moment. There was something about Noah's personality and his energy that made everyone fall in love with him. Noah and his sister were the only children during that time in my mother's house, so its safe to say they received all the love and attention they needed.

My two youngest siblings were living in the house during that time, they had a very close relationship with Noah and his older sister. Whenever I needed a babysitter, I could always count on my youngest brother to keep an eye on them. My youngest brother enjoyed playing games with them, taking them out in the back yard to pick cherries or just simply watch cartoons with them. I watched my baby grow and crawl. As the months went by, he always seemed to be way ahead in my eyes. To hear him uttering his first word: "Mama," the feeling again all so familiar warmed my heart. Noah was not a typical baby that would wake up at nights, at the age of three to four months he started sleeping through the nights. I was very blessed knowing that God had given me one of the best gifts I could have asked for and that was having two healthy and happy children.

Noah was baptized on his 1st birthday, as family and friends gathered for this special occasion, Noah was baptized at Revival Times Tabernacle church in Toronto. Afterwards, we celebrated with a reception at my mother's house; it was a perfect day to celebrate these joyous occasions together. There wasn't a better way for a party to celebrate this little baby with the names of prophets. Family and friends gathered as they will usually do for any special event in my family. Sunday was always a busy day at my mother's house with her traditional soul food dinners. My memory of that was always a warm feeling when walking towards the front door smelling the aroma from the end of the driveway. Noah's christening ceremony was special, I can recall the day as though it was yesterday. We had a private ceremony service at the end of regular church service. The minister was very prophetic when he gave his sermon. I can hear him speaking into Noah's life, I didn't quite understand at the time what he was preaching however I remember my tears pouring out. In the end I was clear on his message. My baby Noah was dressed in his white tuxedo suit and white shoes, he looked as though he was a baby angel. The minister was speaking positive words into Noah's life that day I will always speak about it whenever I'm reminded of that day. He spoke in such a way as if he was certain and sure what God had planned for Noah.

Noah's older sister had been baptized by the same minister as well around the same age of Noah and I don't recall leaving the service the way I did with Noah's, feeling so filled with the message that was delivered. I've never cried during a baptism ceremony; however, I cried a lot at the time of Noah's christening. I recall the minister saying to me "I need you to stop crying and asking God why?" It felt as though he was reading my mind. I stood there as I held my head up looking at the minister holding my son on my hip. My body experienced feeling hot and cold within a short span of time, I can feel my arm pits getting sweaty at this point, my heart increased with every beat. At first, I didn't understand what the minister was preaching about, but he must have known the pain I was experiencing during the service. It was a pain that I had caused myself. I had my family and close friends around to support me, but the one person I wanted there wasn't present, the father of my son. The choices that I had made earlier affected that. It didn't stop what I was doing concerning my son, I had made the best decisions based on the cards I had in my hands. I decided to walk by faith and not by sight and to hold my head up no matter the outcome.

Leaving Noah's ceremony that day, I knew that God had already received him into His house. I truly felt that he was delivered to Him in spirit from a young age. I felt as though he was loaned to me for a period and I was blessed with an angel leaving church that day.

I didn't realize a year had gone by so quickly while home taking care of my children until Noah turned one. At this point my baby was walking and trying to speak all at the same time. Just like any other christening lots of photos were taken, family members and friends gathered at my mother's house, in the west end of Toronto. The house was filled with lots of soul food, laughter and good music, everyone had a merry time. I remembered ordering a "blue clues" character cake for Noah, it was his favourite cartoon character at the time. He loved blowing out the candles on his cake and sticking his tiny hands on the edge of the cake smudging the icing and licking of his fingers afterwards. That Sunday was a memorable event for the entire family, the afternoon turned out great, after all the planning and preparation, Noah enjoyed his birthday celebration and christening surrounded by family that loved and adored him.

What I learned during this chapter:

During this point in my life, I learned so much about myself. Becoming a mother at a young age I embraced and accepted all the changes and challenges that came with it. I also learn not to judge a book by its cover, sometimes you can look at someone and think things are great with them based on how they present their outward appearance, but you don't know what's happening on the inside - how much pain they might be experiencing and what they have gone through. I learnt to give a helping hand whenever I would see someone in distress and need and I learnt to remember that situations could be worse. God had his hands covering me during those times, he always did, and he always will. I learned at a very young age never to give up and to be true to myself. I learned what its like to be loved and to love. With each of my pregnancies, the birth of my children has brought a different type of joy into my life. To hear them say their first words, "Mama," that always melted my heart. I have a different view on life and have always kept in the back of my head that I'm someone's mother and they are depending on me. They are and will always be my reason why.

CHAPTER THREE

Here's to a new beginning moving away
from a busy city to a quiet suburban
neighbourhood and a difficult decision I
had to make for Noah and his sisters.

IT WAS TIME for me to move from the busy life in Toronto, I always imagined living in a quiet neighbourhood when raising my kids. I spent most of my teenage years in the busiest part of the west end of Toronto, so I wanted more for them. I did not want them to see and have the same experiences as I did. I made a conscious decision to move to Woodbridge Ontario, North of Toronto so that we could experience a better lifestyle. When we moved to Woodbridge, Noah attended daycare from a young age until he was ready to attend school. He attended "Centered on Children" Daycare Centre for his JK year program instead of going to a regular school. While attending there he was loved by all the teachers that knew him and those who encountered him. He was known for being funny and being a ladies' man! Noah was known for always complimenting the teachers that worked there and for always having something good to say to them. Noah enjoyed going to the park at the daycare and climbing on the slides and playing with other kids on the playground.

While attending daycare, it was noticed that Noah appreciated art. Painting was one his favourite things to do, he always wanted in on any activity that had paint and coloring involved.

One of Noah's favourite daycare teachers he had and loved dearly was Miss Sabrina. He loved her like she was his one of his family members. That wasn't unusual at the daycare. The experience you had at the daycare was a feeling of being at home in a huge house filled with family members. The teachers were nurturing and attentive to the kids and the parents. The meals were prepared and served with love; this was Noah's other favourite part of daycare! He loved and enjoyed lunch. One of his favourite meals here was pasta and meat balls. I can go on and on, back to his favourite teacher, He always talked about her whenever I will pick him up from daycare, he will mention to me on the drive home what Sabrina did, what games they played at daycare and what book she read to him. Everyday I heard a fresh story regarding Sabrina, I recall one day dropping him to daycare one morning and that day I guess he knew Sabrina was wearing a new fragrance, he ran and gave her a hug as usual, then he says to her: "I like your perfume Sabrina!" She looked at him and smiled and said, "Thanks Noah It's a new fragrance I bought" Noah was a charmer; he would smile, and her face will just be lit up. He always enjoyed daycare knowing that one of his favourite teachers was there. Noah's older sister attended school and the same daycare for the afterschool program, and they spent a lot of time together on the playground.

Noah was the little baby brother she loved and protected but that wasn't for too long, he was no longer going to be the baby. I was now expecting my third child; Noah and his older sister were going to be older siblings. As you can imagine my pregnancy with my third was different just like the rest, but I love every stage of pregnancy and enjoyed being pregnant again and bringing my baby into the world like my other two children. Noah always liked little babies, but he grew more love from just liking his little sister, he loved and admired her. His baby sister attended the same daycare as well, she was two years younger than him. She was just down the hall from him in another classroom. They both were inseparable, same type of bonding he had with his older sister. He loved her so much! He was so nurturing and gentle with her. Noah loved little babies, he liked the idea of being a big brother and that he was his little sister's protector. After moving to Woodbridge, I realised very quickly that it was one of the best decisions I could have made for my kids and myself. I worked in the same area twenty minutes from where I lived and ten minutes to the daycare and school. The set up was perfect for my family, I was driving and had a vehicle to get me different places quickly. I was happy at my job and the field I was working in and for once I was happy overall. Things started turning in the right direction.

Having three kids now though, made things a bit more challenging. I had more on my plate to take on daily. Anyone who has multiple children knows, you have less time for yourself, while a working a full-time job, trying to balance different age groups, dealing with school, homework and much more. I mastered it the best I could. There were days that went by where I wished I had 36 hours in a day. I spent every hour trying to utilize it down to the minute. No time was ever wasted, and other days felt like it was longer because there was more to do. Noah graduated from his daycare when he completed JK. It was so pleasant to see how fast he was growing into a bright boy. I was proud of that moment and was excited for more to come. Every moment I saw him excel brought me great joy.

It was the 1st day of SK. Noah was now attending school with his older sister. He had been talking about going to "big school" all summer long, he had visited the school on the playground during the summer for him to get familiarized with his surroundings. We lived just five walking minutes from the school, so he would always run up to the school whenever talking a walk in that direction to the park. On the first day of school in September I remember seeing his face and how excited he was; his bag pack was bigger than him and he had the smile on his face as if he's a big boy now ready for "big school". Just like every other first day of school I would drop my kids off and watch them as they walked into the gates. That morning I dropped his younger sister off to daycare and took Noah with his older sister to school. I watched them both walk into the school grounds as they met their teachers inside the gated waiting area. Seeing that it was Noah's first day of school for SK, I watched him from the fence as he walked into the school, it was hard as usual to see him go off into someone else's care. I cried; but it was happy tears. I realized how quickly he was growing up in front of my eyes. My baby boy was grown and no longer the little baby I took home from the hospital.

After dropping them off to school I headed to work. I was working at a safety and supply company from 8:30am-5:00pm. The schedule was perfect for my lifestyle with the children. Things were right where they needed to be. One day I was at work and I received a phone call from Noah's school. Noah's teacher had called regarding an incident that happened earlier that day. I thought to myself this must be serious, I remember her telling me that Noah had a rough day at school, he had an incident, where he scratched her on her arm. She went on telling me that "he was upset about being told what to do and also he wasn't following along in classroom." This was very puzzling to me, however I thought maybe its just a rough day, given that he's still adjusting into a new school setting with a new teacher and its only been a couple of months into the start of school. This was the start of what was coming next. As the months went by, I was receiving phone call after phone call from the school with incident after incident. Some of the calls I had my concerns and others they could have been dealt with at the school level. My belief and my experience were during this time the teachers at that time were having a difficult time understanding him and how he learned best and seemed to forget that each child is different and learns differently. The calls came through frequently at my work on my personal cell phone and on my home phone. Being a single mom again at the time it was difficult for me, managing my children, trying to figure out if there's such a thing as work life balance. I knew I needed to work and maintain a stable job/career. I was also faced with the everyday challenge of physically taking care of my three kids on my own. While I worked, there was a lot of juggling things around trying to make things work out for the best for them. After a numerous amount of calls around Noah's "conduct," I decided to discuss the issues that had arisen with Noah's father.

Noah's father played a very important role in his life. He loved his father dearly and looked up to him as his superhero. Noah would frequently visit his dad on the weekends, during holidays and school breaks. His father and I talked about the issues, concerns and the challenges that I was experiencing, and he decided that he would step in and help when the time was right. I also had a babysitter that was living at home assisting in helping me, with some of my daily activities and tasks concerning my children. She would assist with the prepping meals and making sure the kids were up in the morning and getting them out the door for school. She was great sitter and helped tremendously. The sitter had come from the Caribbean to work for me, however it didn't take long before she decided she did not want to be a nanny any longer and she ended walking out on me unexpectedly, without warning. I was at work one day and the kids were attending school and daycare, I came home that evening from work after picking up my kids from daycare. When I drove up the driveway the house was still in darkness, I figured she must be watching television or taking a mini nap before we get home. As I proceeded to open the door, something didn't seem right there was nothing but silence. I called her name as I shuffled my children and myself into the house. No one answered or came to the front door to greet me and my kids. I took off their jackets and shoes without even hanging them up, I tossed them onto the chair in the living room then proceeded upstairs to check the rest of the house. I checked all the rooms and bathrooms she was not there, lastly, I checked her room. As I entered the room, I looked around; the closet door was open, and I noticed all her clothing was gone. The closet was completely empty. I headed downstairs and went into the kitchen and as I entered into the kitchen, I noticed there was an unfolded letter on the counter top, hand written in black ink pen. I realised that she had written a message for me. In the letter, she basically described the reasons why she could not continue to work anymore as a sitter and that she had left to pursue her dreams amongst other things. I was in shocked as to how and when she left and worried about her safety, as she had not been in the country for long, at most only five months. I trusted that the sitter would have been a great help with my children and knew at that time with her being here things would have been less hectic going forward. Once again, I was now doing it all on my own, as a single mother working full time and having my children in daycare and school. Days, weeks went by with the struggle to balance it all. I recall taking naps during the weekend when I was home on a Saturday with the kids, whenever they went down for their midday naps I was also ensuring that I slip one in, that way I can manage and cope for the rest of the day without feeling overwhelmed and exhausted. I didn't know how taking the naps was going to last, as much as it was great for me and my children, because I was falling behind in my work at home. Managing to do laundry, grocery shopping, cleaning and so forth, was becoming very stressful and overwhelming. However, I balanced it and managed the best that I could without over working myself at the time.

At that point, I had to make a long-term decision that was intended to be beneficial and healthy for all of us. I had a very open and understanding relationship with Noah's father, we would speak regularly, and he would always have an open mind when it came to what was in the best interests of Noah and my other children. After giving it some thought and considering everything that I was going through at the time, I decided to speak with Noah's father about the struggle that I was experiencing with him (Noah) and I asked if he would assist more physically with Noah, on a weekly basis. His father recognized that I needed the help immediately and it didn't take long for him to decide that he would step up and help more going forward. Noah's father and I both decided to make the mutual decision to have Noah live with him for two years. The plan was that Noah would return home when he turned six. I initially thought that this sounded like a good option, but on the other hand I wrestled with the thought of not having him at home with his sisters. While I only wanted what was best for him, fear and anxiety came over me. I thought about all the great things he can accomplish while he was with his father. I rationalised that Noah would only be twenty-five to thirty minutes drive away from home. I knew I would see him on a regular basis, and that not much would change except for the fact that he would not be at home during the week. I also knew that Noah always wanted to stay longer with his dad after spending the weekend and school breaks with him, even though it would be unbelievably hard for me to let Noah go and live with his dad for two years. I had to make a very difficult decision and prayed that all things would work out for the best for everyone. I revisited all the pros, time and time again in my mind. The fact that Noah would have that father and son bond, he would get to visit his grandmother frequently and would be able to build a relationship with his brothers. During this time, I didn't have the luxury or the option of quitting my job, if I had done that, I would have been unable to provide for myself and my children, and the idea of being on welfare wasn't appealing. I couldn't possibly stay home waiting to receive maybe twelve hundred dollars to feed and to take care of a family of four. I wanted more not just for my children but also for myself. I would pray about any move and any decision before making them and I always asked God to direct me.

The decision to send Noah to live with his father was one of the hardest decisions I ever had to make. I remember sitting Noah down to inform him that he was going to live with his father on a temporary basis, I told him that his father and I had decided that it was going to be for two years and that then he would return home. After having the conversation with Noah, he was happy about it, he was happy that he would get to go and live with his dad, while still visiting us on a regular basis and he knew that it was only going to be temporary for him. He was not only happy to be with his father, but also, he had a step brother that he loved and talked about constantly and an older brother on his father side whom he looked up to. It was a good setting for Noah to form a bond with his brothers and father.

It was Noah's moving day, I packed his bags and got him ready, I recall his face being so happy, and a bit sad on the other side that he was leaving us. I assured him that he will not be far from us and it was only thirty minutes drive into Toronto to get to him. He did not want to leave his sisters especially his baby sister. When his sisters were informed and knew about him moving, they were very sad to see him leave home, they talked about their play in the evening and how much they would miss that as well as the daycare morning drop offs, and evening pick up when I would pick them up. There was never a dull moment in the house with them together. His older sister was very positive about it, she would tell Noah that it was only going to be temporary until Mommy gets more help, she would also tell him that she will see him on the weekends and that it will be more fun that way, instead of him having visits with his father over the weekends. She made her little brother felt very comfortable about him living there as though she was a mother herself. My heart ached every step of the way throughout the whole process leading up to the day when it was time to take him to his father's house. This was one of the hardest moments of my life. I remember taking Noah's bag to the car along with his favourite Sponge Bob blue and yellow fleece blanket, he would always sleep with this blanket. We drove to his dad's home. When we arrived, Noah greeted his dad with a big hug! I remember his dad saying to me: "don't worry he's in good hands, not to worry!" I knew Noah's dad was a great father to his eldest son also his eldest son had lived with him when he was much younger. I knew also that Noah would have a step brother and his older biological brother to hang out with. Noah had the best of both worlds.

What I learned during this chapter:

I learned that life has its ups and downs, with every growing stage you will have difficulties and it is what you do during those difficult times that will shape your future. There will also be challenges and changes along the way, some of which you will not be comfortable with. You must make the best decision for you and your immediate family. Think about the positives and the negatives that will arrive from the situation and if the good outweighs the bad then make your decisions based on that. For every disappointment you will be rewarded.

Be gentle with yourself, take time out for you, you're all you have.

CHAPTER FOUR

Noah transitions into his new home at his father's residence, A turning point in my life and in Noah's.

NOAH WAS NOW living at his father's home getting familiar with his surroundings, new rules, new family dynamics and adjusting to his new school setting. He attended a local public school in the neighbourhood which was less than four minutes walk from home. He was making new friends both in school and outside of school in the surrounding neighbourhood. His grandmother also lived in the same building. He spent a lot of time before and after school with his grandmother and attended church on Sundays with her as well, if he was home with her. He truly loved and cared for her dearly. She was everything for Noah and she did nothing wrong in Noah's eyes. Noah also enjoyed attending the flea market with her occasionally to help her set up and sell her goods. Not only did he enjoy that, his favourite hobby to do with her was to go shopping. I would hear all the stories when Noah visited me on the weekends of what they bought and how long they stayed in the stores. As much as he sounded like he was complaining, he loved every moment of it. Not to mention them going out to eat at one of his favourite restaurants, Mandarin, and when she would make his favourite cornmeal porridge. My time with Noah was reversed now, I went from having him during the week to seeing him on the weekends, holidays and school breaks. Even though it was a very hard transition for my family I made the best of our situation. I was grateful for the time we spent together with Noah; it worked out for us, most weekends were filled with fun activities such as going to the movies, the arcade and or just relaxing at home enjoying each other's company. We appreciated the little things more about each other and valued the time we spent together.

The first semester started and was over, and time was passing by very quickly. Noah had spent the summer with us just as planned. I was so excited to have him home, I missed him so much. I missed hearing the simple things, like hearing his voice in the house and listening to him chatter with his sisters. I didn't realize how hard it was for me at first to not have him there with us. I made the best of our summer months together, taking advantage of the hot sunny days, spending our time in theme parks and just forming a different type of relationship with him. It felt like I was getting to know and learn about him all over again. Things weren't the same without having him around on a regular basis. We had done so much throughout the summer I didn't want any it to end, because I knew he would be going back to be with his dad for another school year. The day that he left I was already counting down the time from since he left to when he was coming back home. The feeling I had every night going to bed was intense, there was always that void I had, a void that was just lingering throughout each day that passed. September came around again and it was another school year for Noah, Grade One, he was still attending at his new school that he started in Toronto. He had gotten accustomed to his routine, friends and his new school. Noah had made a lot of new friends, he was doing great in new school, there were still the regular challenges that any parent had to deal with however there were fewer phone calls from the school to his father. His dad and his grandmother were working closely with Noah and were helping him to achieve great results in every area of his life. I heard great things from Noah at nights when he would call me before going to bed. I looked forward to the phone calls, it was my only calm at the end of my long days. Sometimes I would just listen to him breathing on the other end of the phone, those were the times when he didn't have much to say, but still wanted to remain on the call. For me it was comforting to know that he was on the other end and that he had my ear ready to listen to him.

We were now at 1 ½ years in, with Noah still at his father's residence. Things were still going great on his side.

I was on the count down still. Not just for Noah coming home on the weekends but also for him returning home permanently. I was getting used to taking care of my other two children and it was becoming less challenging for me. It felt as though I had mastered juggling and balancing work. I was looking toward Noah returning home but for some reason the time was going by even slower now. We planned and waited in the meantime for his return despite it. I was still working at the safety and supply company in Woodbridge, it was a close family work environment, I was working on a regular Friday evening as usually running reports etc. I recall laughing and talking with my co worker at the time, which was roughly about 4:00pm when an unknown stranger, a man walked into the office and asked for "Natalie Watson". I replied and said, "I'm Natalie Watson". He looked at me and handed me a brown envelope and told me that I've been served on behalf on Noah's Father. My heart dropped instantly the smile and laughter I had on my face before that man came in was completely gone from my face. I thought to myself, served? For what? I've never been to court before or heard of anyone being served court documents by the father of their child. This was new territory for me, I didn't know why he would take me to family court. I went into the bathroom and opened the package in private, I was too embarrassed to do it in front of my co-worker but I'm sure she realized what it was. I recalled reading it and realised very quick that Noah's father was seeking custody of him and seeking child support. I laughed right away because I thought it was some type of joke, but I knew how serious it was. My life was about to change, I knew that the court business was not a walk in the park and I've never gone to court before in my life for anything. I didn't know where to start, so many thoughts ran through my mind. Do I retain a lawyer? How am I going to afford a lawyer? I left work and went home that day feeling low and drained. The energy and life were sucked out of me feeling down and confused at the same time. All this time I've been waiting for Noah's return home, which was just a few months away and I knew that this would slow the process down if I didn't act fast. I was not going to back down. I was ready to give my all just to have my son home where he belonged. I acted quickly to the situation, I started my own digging and investigated my resources and found out that I was entitled to Legal Aid. I hadn't heard of Legal Aid before, but I was ready to see how this would benefit me. Weeks went by and time was approaching for me to attend court. I went in for a review to see if I was qualified and it turned out I was. I was now receiving advice from a lawyer, he was never the greatest attorney and I viewed him as being very relaxed and seemed very new at what he was doing, however he thought my case was simple enough for him to deal with. After our first appearance in court I knew that I had to put up a fight and fight for my son's return home, a fight that I've never fought before. I was determined to have my son back home with me. No one was going to tell me otherwise. Two years had gone by and it approached on us so fast, Noah was still in his father's care and I felt like I was just fighting a losing battle with him. All along

I thought it would be an easy transition home like how it had been when he went to his dad's house. My thoughts were wrong, and my hope seemed too high. After the 2-year mark to be exact, I remember crying at nights in bed just to have Noah home. I did not let Noah see any of my bitter feelings towards his father for what he did. I reminded Noah that his dad and I loved him dearly and we both are trying to decide what would be in his best interests. It wasn't the easiest for Noah to understand but he knew how much we both cared and loved him dearly. Month after month it was challenging going to court to hear a stranger decide on what was best for my son. At this point Noah was now asking when is he going home? I had no definite answers; however, I recall telling him that I was doing everything in my power to have him back home with us. Noah knew that we both loved him dearly and wanted to live with us. We couldn't hide anything from him, he was a very bright child and picked up clues very easily. The months were long and hard. I watched the little boy I knew, who was filled with energy, change right in front of my eyes. Noah wanted to return home sooner than later, but it wasn't happening fast enough for him and time seemed as though it was not on my side. During the court process it felt as if things weren't ever going to end. Each visit was getting more difficult. I was still having visits on the weekend with Noah and I still had no answers for him when he asked the question when was he coming back home? My court dates were spread apart from each other, which didn't help as well. Time was not on my side. I felt helpless and hopeless and

I started thinking how long this is going to take to wrap up. My thoughts were scattered, thinking this cannot be happening to me. How was I going to get out of this new situation I'm in?

What I learned during this chapter:

During this phase of my life I learnt the importance of being strong. When faced with what you might think is the worst news, change your mindset on how you go about handling your situation. Having patience is key, think about how you want things to look like in the end. Instead of focusing on the negative, look at all the positives and let that be your only motivation.

CHAPTER FIVE

Having to be persistent while everything changes within a blink of an eye. From a temporary to a permanent home setting, dealing with custody access and the day to day challenges of life.

I WAS ALWAYS excited when I knew I was going to have my visits with Noah on the weekends, I so looked forward to my weekend visits with him. I wished there were more days to the weekend, it went by far too fast. Even though it was difficult on Sundays, taking him back, I was getting accustomed to the idea of him living at his dad's house permanently, even though I was not going to give up on having him home with his sisters. Noah would continue to ask me questions about when he's coming home, and I would always remind him that I hadn't given up. He was always persistent making sure he asked each time he visited us.

As time went by Noah himself got more adjusted to the idea of living there permanently. Now that he was going to school and had made lots of new friends, he would always talk about his friends, what he did in school during the week and about his new teachers. Noah was involved in sports activities and took swimming lessons while living with his father. He loved and enjoyed swimming. Noah also enjoyed attending the local community centre where he would play basketball and challenge himself with older kids. Sports and outdoor activities were Noah's happy place, he always kept himself occupied involved in things that he enjoyed. If he was active, he was in heaven. Another one of Noah favourite things to do was going to the movies. Noah particularly loved the Marvel movies. Whenever a movie was coming out in the theatre Noah would be the first one to talk about it with his friends and family, he was a huge movie fan and critic. He had great taste in movies. Whenever Noah would visit on the weekends, he would give his sisters an earful with his views and all the movies that he'd seen.

I continued to work at the safety and supply company performing the same duties and continued taking care of my other children living with me. I was now paying child support for Noah, given that Noah was now living with his dad on a permanent basis. The judge had ordered me to pay an amount that was out of my budget and things weren't the greatest on my end financially during this time. I have fallen so many times; my life was never perfect. For you to understand Noah's story and his personality, I must be transparent about myself as Noah's mother.

I have failed at many things in my life that I set out to do. During the time when Noah lived with his father, I made a lot of sacrifices and fell to rock bottom. I was now faced with losing my car and my condo apartment I lived in with my kids. The whole process had taken a mental and a physical toll on me. At this time, I lost my place of residence, I lost my vehicle and with the rate I was going coming in late to work, missing days I was very close in losing that as well. However, for some reason, I managed to keep the job, it kept me focus and positive and I was able to work out my difficulties and the struggles I was having in other areas of my life. It was the only thing going in the right direction for me. I wanted to give up, but I would not, even if I wanted to. My fighting inner spirit would not allow me to surrender. Noah and his sisters were my inspiration and they kept me going. They lit a fire in me that I never knew I had, and I realised that God had other plans for me. Every step of the way God had shown me grace, whenever I had doubts or lack clarity, he would show me there's still a lot to be thankful for. It was my weekend visit to have Noah. I recall that weekend we were driving to our apartment after having a long weekend out. When Noah asked if he can tell me something personal, automatically I replied with a "yes". What he disclosed to me was mind blowing. He continued to tell me that a family member had touched him inappropriately and he didn't like it. I was unbelievably shocked and appalled about what Noah was telling me. I knew right away I had to get to the bottom of this. The feeling of being confused, overwhelmed and panicked with all other mixed emotions. I couldn't think clearly. I was ready that moment to investigate it and find out what was happening. I comforted Noah and told him it would not happen again on my watch and that none of it was his fault. I told a family member that same weekend and brought it to his father's attention at the same time. We discussed the issues and decided that we will not have the two family members alone. His father and I were both in disbelief that a family member would do such a thing. Not knowing exactly where to turn and what to do after sharing the news with a few family members over the weekend. I was worried, anxious and I wanted the matter investigated further. I took matters into my own hands and reached out to (CAS) Children's Aid Society after addressing the issues with his father and not getting results. I knew it was a difficult decision and it was new territory that I was moving into, however I had to do it for the safety of my child. I wanted and needed to know he was safe when he wasn't in my care. I knew in the back of my head that when I opened that can of worms, things would change, it was going to be a process that was long; and I knew it was going to get messy at some point for myself and most importantly for Noah. It didn't take the CAS long before the matter was taken further. I was now in and out of court regularly, it was a lengthy and daunting process for both Noah and me. To make an incredibly and lengthy year-long process inside and outside of court short, the ultimate decision was CAS didn't have enough evidence to charge that family member. The process was not the easiest and I hated it every step of the way for many reasons. Not only did it take a toll on me, but it also deeply affected Noah's sisters and Noah himself. A lot had transpired during that time and I knew things would never be the same going forward with my son. We returned to court with CAS and during that time, I was able to get through the process without having to hire a lawyer. The goal was to address all the allegations against that family member. I was prepared despite of the outcome. I had faith in believing Noah that he was telling the truth. Things were settled again or seemed to be somewhat. Noah and I grew a special bond from me believing in him and showing up for him in court every step of the way. I assured him and kept my promise that I would be there for him, no matter the outcome and what life may throw at us. I would always have his back and his sisters. At that point my relationship started taking a turn for the better with Noah. He knew that he could say anything to me, and he trusted me more.

With my personality and perseverance, I had developed great faith. I was able to build myself up from accepting the news of Noah's permanent home again. I always knew that God would work everything out for the good for my family, I prayed, and I was very persistent also. I never doubted one bit that Noah would not be home permanently again, but it was hard for me to accept the news as a mother after what my son had disclosed to me and his experience. Noah and I are alike we had the same fighter's personality and drive, and often other family members would tell me that we were alike in so many ways. People would say that Noah reminded them of me when I was much younger. There was nothing in the world that is too big or small that we couldn't handle. Noah wasn't afraid to return home, he hadn't been afraid to tell someone what had happened and throughout the whole process it was very brave. Everyone involved discussed our concerns after everything was settled in court. We all knew what was expected of us from all aspects. The months went by without us hearing any worries or concerns from Noah, he was ok settling back after all that happened and the lengthy legal process that he had to experience. The situation was not easy for him, given that it was a close family member who was involved. Noah had mixed emo-tions about everything and worried about his relationship with them going forward. As the time passed, he also got comfortable, confident and continued being open with me, his sisters and his father. Noah also voiced his concerns and believed that a similar incident occurred with a female babysitter. Talk about bravery from Noah. He had a voice, he stood up and speak up for himself without hesitation, there wasn't much taken care of in this case, we were unable to locate the young teenager's whereabouts so it didn't go as how we would have liked. Noah was able to deal with it by thinking positive thoughts, without blaming himself and received the help experiencing such trauma. It wasn't an easy fix for him at first, but he got through it each day one step at a time. Months turned into years and time was going by. Life continued to happen for our family. Noah's two sisters were getting older and I was now expecting my fourth child. Noah was going to be a big brother to another little sister. Noah loved babies and he fell in love with his new little baby sister the minute he knew he was having a sibling. His new sister brought a lot of joy to Noah. She was now Noah's first favourite and his middle sister being his second. Having Noah home on the weekends meant he was always looking forward to now being in his baby sister's company. He enjoyed giving her lots of hugs and kisses. My life was coming together in a good way, there were lots of positive and exciting things for our family, good changes and new ones too. Well I thought things were going well but as usual I've learned not to get too comfortable.

Just when I thought things were ok and Noah had finally adjusted to his home setting and living with his father, one day, while I was home, I received the worst news any mother could hear or imagine. I recall being at home in the kitchen preparing dinner after a long day, when I received a phone call to come and get Noah from the police station. I dropped everything and stopped what I was doing. I got into my car and remembered driving for roughly thirty minutes to Toronto. I'm not sure how I got there so fast, but I did. I had called my brother on the way down and told him to meet me there and told him that there had been an emergency with Noah. I finally arrived at the station, it was close to sunset at this point, as it was roughly 8:30pm on a June summer night. I recall that school was almost out for summer break. As I walked into the police station my body was cold and my heart was beating out of control at a rapid, uncontrollable rate. I was greeted with by a CAS case worker in the lobby area of the building. The same case worker that we had worked with roughly a year ago on the previous case. She looked as if she was very disappointed. I asked her immediately if Noah was ok, she replied "yes" in a very stern way. I was then greeted by a police officer, who let me know right away that all was well with Noah. As I sat down and heard the news this time, there were allegations around physical discipline. I knew my life would change drastically when I heard the news and so it did. After I was briefed on the incident at the station, I was able to see Noah. They had him in another room waiting for me. I recall seeing him and he how he looked stressed and as if he just needed to go home. I rushed into the room to get to him. My heart had never felt so empty and broken before, as I stretched my arms out and gave him the biggest hug, I felt the pain as a mother. I just wanted everything to be over with. I was in that motion again of just wanting him to come home and be home. There was too much that went on within such a short span of time. Noah had tears in his eyes and with one blink his tears flowed down his cheeks. That night the CAS worker allowed me to take Noah home, until she sorted out a few things on her end. Due to Noah's father having custody I couldn't just take him back home without going through the legal way to gain back custody. Without hesitation I was more than happy to have him back home with me, even if it were for a night, or an extra week, more time with me under the circumstances was ideal. I wanted it all to stop, this nightmare and roller coasters of events seems to just linger. I knew it would be another year of paperwork and back in court system. The thought of it all was exhausting and not appealing with the other experiences I've had. I dreaded the idea of going down that road again. My brother finally arrived and met me at the station, worried and frantic after riding his bike down. I filled him in on what had happened, he was shocked and upset, not just because of what had happened, but because he knew of the previous incident. My brother wanted to know when it would stop for Noah, when would things reach a breaking point and when I would also get a break from all that had been going on within the last 2 years plus. At this point I was in tears, ready again to put up the fight for Noah. Even though I felt like "This is it! I'm giving up! I cannot take it any longer," I couldn't surrender. I was weary and tired, tired of having to fight for what I believe in should happened in the best interest of my child, but I had to still fight for safety, fight for survival. All around I was broken and wasn't sure how I was going to get through this level of stress again. Each time I would pray, and I would ask God to help me and get me through and He always does. I wasn't too sure how I was going to overcome this one. I thought to myself that God is probably tired of hearing from me. I keep asking Him and He's always had my back and here I am asking again. To be honest, I never stopped asking. It was such a long day and night for Noah and me at the station. I took Noah and went back to my house, with his school clothes on and backpack from school. That day I knew he was just ready for bath and bed. On the way to my house I reassured him he was safe, and he felt a bit more at ease.

I didn't really have a plan or idea of where to start but I knew I couldn't watch him slip through my fingers again. This time I was in charge and in control, I had confidence and prayed for change. There was a fire that was lit inside of me again, a fire like never. Noah and I finally made it home safe that night, his sisters waited up for us that night. We were both tired at this point. Usually, I would just send Noah into the shower but that night I ran a bath for him and filled the tub with warm water. I helped him by washing him from head down. As I wash his back, he was tense and sore. I cried with every touch of water that was running down his body from the bath. Noah was crying also. I can tell as a mother of four and as his mother he was not his usual self. As he sat in the bath of water, he kept telling me what happened. All I could do at that time, was listen and reassure him that he was safe and was not to worry any more. I promised him that he would no longer have to live with that situation. My heart ached so much with a pain as though it was menstrual pain or the pain from having contractions while giving birth. I stared at him for a long time in the bath. Feeling hopeless and lifeless and not sure what I was going to do. I didn't understand and could not accept the thought of a family doing this to my son. I had so many questions, that I will never know the answers to. The following day my Fiancé and I had to take Noah to the hospital to be examined. As I sat in the waiting room, I watched Noah play with the books and toys that were there in the corner. I overheard the conversations from other patients and doctors. There were other people that were coming and going on the floor. So many thoughts ran through my mind it felt as if I was in a movie or a terrible dream that I couldn't wake up from. Not to mention I didn't sleep from the night before; I had stayed up plotting and planning how to get through this time. I knew after listening to the conversations around me that I was the only person that was going through this.

When I heard Noah's name, I knew it was our turn to go in and see the doctor. As we were walking towards the examination room, my heart skipped a beat. I was scared, felt nauseated and terrified. I've never felt this pain, anxiety and confusion before. As I sat off to the side in the room and observed Noah's examination, I can see the tears set up in his eyes. every pain that he felt, my little baby - I felt it all. I can still hear myself telling him: "It's ok Nonoe," a nickname that I had for him, "they're checking you to make sure that you're ok." I kept calling him Nonoe. The echoes of my voice in the room bouncing off the plain white walls as I call him by his nickname. Noah had black and blue marks on his arms and legs, they were more obvious and visible under the doctor's light than they had been the night before. Everything was checked carefully, and Noah was cleared to be ok from the doctor. I was relieved to hear from the doctor that he was checked out good. It had been a very long and overwhelming day for Noah.

A few days went by with Noah now in my care, he knew he was home and safe, and he was adjusting well with his sisters. It didn't take much for Noah to smile again. He enjoyed going to the park with his friends that he had in our neighbourhood. Noah made friends wherever he went.

It was two weeks now since Noah was living back home with me and his sisters, he was in a good routine and enjoying the time he had with his sisters. Things seemed to be on track, but Noah experienced some rough withdrawals, due to being away from his father. He had been with him for some years and was used to being with his father and in school, with all his friends. Noah received counselling for all the trauma he had experienced within such a short period of time. I did everything in my power to see that he would be ok again. I attended drop in sessions on parenting classes that would equip me with more knowledge on how to best deal with Noah. I knew he was not the same child, just by what I was seeing in his adjustment at home and behaviour, but he was still coping well overall. Just when I thought things were working out for the best and in the direction, they should be going, I got a call from the CAS worker that Noah's father wanted custody back. I couldn't believe what I was hearing, after all that had happened. She also mentioned that we would have to go to court again to reassess the custody agreement. This time going back into court would be myself against CAS and his father. I was faced with my worst nightmare again. Court! I hated the word when ever I heard it, and here I was, not only going back in against his father but now also against the CAS.

Here I am again in court, it all seems familiar this time around. I sit in the waiting room on the first appearance date in court. I couldn't believe I was here again.

Thinking when all this would just stop. I had a story to tell my son when he gets older. All the trial and tribulations that I experienced I knew God was preparing me for greatness, something beyond what I couldn't imagine. I sat there, and my soul was just tired and weary again. Praying to God to help me out of this mess again. I didn't know what else to do and I had no one and no where else to turn, even if I wanted to hide, there was no where to hide from it all. It was almost as if I were fighting a war that was never ending. But somewhere at the back of my mind I knew that this too shall pass. It was our turn to enter the court room. This time around I felt somewhat prepared compared with my first appearance years ago. I was able to speak with more confidence and surety but all that didn't seem to matter to CAS, his father or the judge. CAS had other plans, those plans were to take Noah into care and my son's father's allegations that I was an "unfit mother" was not helping the circumstances or in my favour. Everything was working against me, I had Noah living with me and he was about to slip right through my fingers again. I had Noah's three other sisters living with me, if they thought that I was that horrible of a parent or "unfit" what would stop them from taking them from me too? Everything happened so fast, within a blink of an eye, the judge made her decision after being in the court room for roughly 15-20 minutes. A decision that would affect everyone's lives, not only my life, but also Noah's dad's and his sisters; everyone that knew what was happening. The judge made the decision and ordered that Noah be taken into care. I sat in the court room and cried, I was so shocked at how could they decide so fast and I could not figure out whose interest this was in? How was I going to break this horrible news to Noah? This day was one of the most depressing days of my life. CAS had got what they asked for. I could not understand how it got to this point. They decided that they would take Noah from my house that same day and place him into care into a stranger's home. The system can work for you and against you. There was no valid reason for this drastic decision, but it was now out of my control and out of my hands. As soon as I was dismissed from the court room, I hurried home again. Before I could get to my house, I called my sister that was living down the street from me at the time and asked that she go to my house until I get there. As soon as I arrived at my house, Noah's grandmother on his father's side, who was in court when we heard the news, also came back to my house with my Fiancé and I. I wanted to get home as soon as possible, before the CAS worker arrived and to spend the time with Noah to let him know what was going to happen. Everyone was spooked and shocked by the news. We were all frantic and in disbelief at what had happened. After getting to my house I didn't know the best way to break the news to Noah, so I did what I had to do in the best way possible. I told him it was a temporary decision and the reason why they decided it, they thought it was best at the time. This was hard news for Noah to receive that day, as I sat him down to tell him I couldn't hold back on my tears at this point, but my family and other children were there to support him too. Noah had already met the case worker, not that it should be easy, but he knew who was coming to pick him up. He remembered her from the police station. She wasn't a stranger taking him directly. It was so very difficult for him having to leave, despite any explanation that was given to him. We all hugged and held Noah tight one after each other. I recall giving him a Bible and told him to pray about what he wants God to answer for him, and that he should turn to Him for comfort. I didn't know what else I could have told Noah at that time to comfort him. This was the only comfort I felt I could have given him at that point.

What I learned during this chapter:

During this chapter of my life, I learned that your faith will be tested in many ways. Never to give up what you believe in even if it means to lose friends and family along the way. When I was informed with the news I received from my son and, the phone call to get my son at a local police station, I felt at that point it will be the end of me. It felt as though those incidents were going to be my breaking point. I learned later that they didn't break me, it was preparing me with what is next in store. Each obstacle and advert I was faced with I learned to pick myself up and keep moving forward no matter what.

CHAPTER SIX

Failure, Family and Faith.
Dealing with failure from family, failure
from the system and almost losing
faith during the midst of it all.

EVEN THOUGH THE system failed me and my family, I still had faith that I would get through it with Noah. Noah was now living with a new family with the same ethnic background and in a Christian home. A few weeks had gone by where I didn't get a chance to see him, but I looked forward to receiving his phone calls at nights. I missed hearing his voice in the house and having his presence at home. Whenever I spoke to Noah, I always asked him if he were safe and comfortable. He would always say to me: "everything is ok mom - the foster caretaker is very nice to me." The house was always noisy, I knew there were other kids and Noah had told me that there were other boys his age there as well. Noah would always ask about his sisters and want to know how everyone else was doing. I wanted to just take him and run away with him far away as possible. It was now three weeks since Noah moved into this new home setting, and I was having a visit with him during the weekday. I couldn't wait for this visit to happen, I looked forward to seeing him after such a long three-week process of waiting and planning. It was a day during the middle of the week, I recall meeting Noah at a local mall in the west end of the city. There was a Walmart there with a McDonald's attached to it. While I was waiting for Noah's arrival, I had a nervous feeling in my stomach, not knowing what to expect and to know that this was my first time just randomly meeting my own child in a public space. I'll be very honest, I felt as though I was unfit, I felt as though I was a stranger now to him and the thought of him living else where did not settle with me. I couldn't understand and still don't to this point. When we finally met up, we had lunch, walked around the store and talked about everything. He was so calm, too calm. I almost thought that he wasn't interested in returning home. But it was a calmness that he had because he was happy to see me, and he reassured me that things were ok on his end. Noah was adapting very quickly; he made the best out of what he had. I now started seeing him on a regular and consistent basis, now that he was somewhat settled in. He was back to the weekend sleep over from Friday to Sunday. I hated it still, I hated having to see him leave on Sundays again, but I made the best of the circumstances and prayed for changes to happen. I used the time to spend as much time with him as much as I could. His visits to his father also resumed as well. Noah was happy to have somewhat of a normalcy in his life. It had been a few months since he had seen his dad, so he looked forward to his time spent with him as well. Whenever I would have my visits with him, he would talk about how much he misses us and tell me about his experience at his current residence. Noah was strong throughout the whole process of going through such a huge move and still looked for the positive in everything that was presented in front of him. I was very proud of him. Not many kids can experience what he had gone through and still have a huge personality like his; but for me on the other hand the time was not going by quickly enough. I couldn't get comfortable with the thought of having him in another person's house and not home with us. I thought it was ridiculous that I had to show that I could take care of Noah, I had three other children in my care and was already taking care of them. I didn't understand why I needed to prove that I was able to care for him? My friends and family members will attest to this as well, this was a shock for my entire family and a new experience for each of us to go through. I was still signed up for parenting classes that I continued going to, it helped me a lot with new views and insights on how to be supportive when dealing with children who had gone through trauma. Other parents attended the weekly sessions as well. Some of these parents would share their stories and experiences that they had had and different methods that they had used to help them get through. I realize very quickly I wasn't alone. I was getting good feedback from the Caseworker; she had said that this would help the process of getting him back sooner. It was all pointless in my opinion, at this point, I didn't care what it was going to take to get him back, I was ready to give everything and anything within my power to have him home. Even if it was showing my face at these weekly sessions that I didn't agree with.

Some months had gone by, I would say 3-5 months, my patience was running very low and my thoughts were scattered about when things were going to change. Noah was changing in front of my eyes slowly. He would still ask when he is coming back home, but with no definite answers to give him, it was a challenging time for both of us. Noah had already at this point moved from two foster homes. The moving started getting to him, he didn't like the idea of changing homes so soon. He was not happy with all the changes in such a short span of time, even though now he was only minutes away from my home. The purpose of the last move was to have him attend the same school as his sister and be closer to home when he transitioned back into our home. During the process of Noah living in care there was planning in place to have one of my family members take him to live with her until I gained full custody back. Meetings were held, and the plans and preparation were in place for him to stay with her. It was close to a year at this point of Noah being in care. I was desperate for the help. Like any other mother, I would have done anything and everything to see him home with me. This was ideal; my family member only lived walking distance away from my home and the school, and the situation would have been ideal for Noah. It wasn't too far into the planning when she made the decision that she could no longer do it for personal reasons. Noah didn't know of this plan, I didn't want to crush him if it didn't work out. It would have been more of a surprise for him if it had worked out. My heart was destroyed by the news after hearing that the plan was not going through, but I had to respect her decision and her reasoning behind it. The only thing that mattered to me at this point was to have Noah out of the current situation he was in. I was focused and driven with fire inside of me to go all the way through to continue fighting for Noah. The time seemed to go by slowly and things were very hard, I really felt like giving up again and let the system have it their way, I came very close to a point where I felt completely hopeless and helpless. At that time, it did feel like the nightmare I was living in was never ending, but I knew I had no room to give up. If I did then that meant that I would end up losing Noah to the system. I didn't want that to be his story and his life. I prayed a lot during these times asking God to help me and take away the sadness it brought to my life and my children life also, but God kept me going when I felt all hope is lost and, in those times, when I was defeated and couldn't see a way out. Somehow, I manage to pick myself up again and continued the fight. Instead of looking for a family member to take Noah, a year had already gone by. My focus was now to get him back. Court dates were stretched out so far from each other, it was good and bad for us at the same time, good because I had time to prepare for the next date and to also gather us much info as I would need before appearing before the Judge and CAS. However, during the waiting process, I made use of all the time. I worked on myself and my relationship with my kids, especially Noah. He was still seeing a counselor to help him, I had accessed a lot of resources for myself and fiancé to help us, that way when we were granted custody, we would be ready. All things were flowing at a smooth pace for Noah at this point. He knew he would be coming home eventually. He was more confident than I ever was that it would all come to an end. Noah was excelling in track and field at school. He enjoyed running, and still enjoyed other sports such as basketball. Basketball was Noah's favourite sport. I recall him at his middle school playing and challenging the gym teacher. He was always up to challenge someone. He thought he was the best at the game. Noah would always say that when he grew up, he wanted to be a basketball player or an architect, he wanted to draw blueprints for major companies. That's when he started focussing more on his drawing and the neatness of it. I recall always telling him that if he wants to be successful at anything, he must give it his best. Noah also enjoyed watching a good game of football, he would watch his dad play on the weekends. He would always brag and say how his dad is "wicked" at football, that was his definition of great. I don't understand the game, but Noah seems to have it all figured out. At this point I was deep into planning for Noah to return home,

I was living in a townhome at the time. I knew eventually that Noah would return and would need his own room and space at some point. I started looking into different areas for a suitable home for my family size. During my search for homes I had another friend who was looking for houses at the same time, and she had mentioned to me that she had heard of houses out in Niagara and that we should take the drive out there. We both ended up in the Niagara region looking for homes. I had already seen a lot of model homes so after visiting with her that day I knew this region was where I wanted to move. It was quiet and away from traffic and all the everyday hassle. When I came back home, I told my fiancé about the homes and he decided that he would take a drive out to see them himself. He came out with me once and we both made the decision that it would be our new home, it didn't take long for us to make the decision to move. We needed more space and the location was ideal for my family. It was a fresh start for us after my fiancé and I got married. I could not wait to gain full custody of him to be in my care and to return home. I was planning a wedding that was to take place outside the country and to celebrate Noah's return home. The August of that same year, we decided to go away as a family to get married. It was the first vacation that Noah had with all of us as a family together and it was the first time, we had all traveled together by plane. We spent 7 days in Dominican Republic, Noah enjoyed himself. He was free spirited and relaxed; this was a new territory for him, and it was a new beginning for more great things to come. Noah enjoyed the beach, the sun and the food. The look that he had on his face daily and how he looked forward to waking up and getting served was perfect for Noah. A lot of time spent on the beach and around the pool with him were great memories that we all shared together as a family. On my wedding day I can see how Noah got emotional when it was his turn to give a speech. He had this big speech planned out, but he couldn't help himself, he cried. For the first time in a long time, he was crying tears of happiness. I could tell he was very happy for our family and happy for me on that day. It melted my heart so much that day to have all my children there with me at last in the moment, happy and excited. The CAS worker had granted me leave to travel outside the country with him for my wedding. A week went by so fast in the Dominican Republic, it seemed as though we had never left Toronto. I didn't want him to come back and go back into care, I wanted our trip to last forever. When I came back from our travels the worker and I were on the same page, she was making her recommendations for Noah to return home, all my praying, planning and having faith was finally getting answered. This was the best news that I could have received in a long time. Noah was told the news, and right away there was a positive change in his demeanor. There were still up and downs and other hurdles we had to go through but overall these were nothing that I couldn't deal with. There was hope for Noah, his father was also in agreement that he should return home. The court date finally came again for us to attend to hear the final decision from the judge. I looked back at each time I had attended court and as time went by with more experience and knowledge gained, I showed up better to represent my family and with more confidence and believed that there's nothing in this world I could not manage.

It was a year and 7 months since Noah was in care. A lengthy unnecessary time. Once again, I was there in court, hearing my name called on the intercom once again to go into the courtroom. It was all familiar to me. I sat there and listened to everything that was being said from others who were wrapping up their case. Then it was my turn. I felt an excitement that I've never had in a courtroom before. I've always had bad news in courtrooms, but today was one of the best days. Again, it didn't take long before the judge made her final decisions. I recall hearing that: "the mother will be awarded custody of the child Noah Watson." A weight was lifted off my shoulders it was the best news I've heard in years. I cried tears of joy and tears of knowing that all the stress would be over. I couldn't wait to leave the court room! All that I wanted to hear was I heard. Noah's father and the worker were pleased with the outcome. For the first time I felt we were all on board and shared the same focus – Noah! With every disappointment and every challenge that I've faced, it was all worth it in the end. However, it was also an experience I would not wish on my worst enemy. I left the courtroom that day smiling as if I had won the Lotto. There was nothing anyone could have done, that would have taken that feeling away from me.

I got home that day and I was pleased to relay the news back to my family. Noah heard the news and I can still see the big bright smile on his face. At the most recent foster home, he was living close to home, so he was over that evening with his sisters. I recall Noah saying to me: "I knew you would not stop until I was home Mom." He didn't have much to say, and was kind of lost for words, but his face alone said it all. I knew there would be a lot of work ahead of me with Noah, but I was up for the challenge. Everything was falling into place with our new home being built. Noah knew that when he moved, he would have his own room for the first time. My family had endured a lot of stress, pain and sacrifice to get to this day. With prayer and perseverance God had seen my family through it all.

What I learned during this chapter:

During this phase of my life: I leaned it is ok to ask for help when you need it. With every disappointment you learn and grow from it. Sometimes when you think you might have it bad, someone might be experiencing a much more difficult situation. I've also learned a lot about my character and the inner strength that I was born with. I didn't know I had such strength and determination until I was faced with difficult decisions to make and others I simply had to live with. My faith was tested weekly and going through each experience, it built me up stronger even when I couldn't see it. looking into this chapter it was one of the most interesting point in my life, going through all the roller coaster of emotions felt never ending. Stepping back and looking at the big picture is always best when your back is against the wall, trust your own judgements if you're doing it from a place of love and care. Other people actions could have dictated the way I respond; however I didn't let that control me, I stay true to myself for what I believe in and stood up for my family even though I knew I will be judged, and talked about. My motivation was my children, they were my number one focus.

CHAPTER SEVEN

A start of a new beginning. Moving to a new region and Noah moving back home permanently.

I STILL COULDN'T believe that I finally had custody of Noah after roughly five years of custody battles. After having been back and forth and in and out of the court system, I felt as though I should have been an expert by now in handling very difficult family law cases.

Noah was finally returning home to my residence. It was a warm day in March when Noah was returned at our home by the case worker, I will always remember and cherish this day. All the pain seemed as though it had come to an end, everything had paid off. I learned a lot throughout the process about the system and myself. I would not wish that anyone else would have to experience "the system," the way that I did, but I somehow got through it all by the grace of God. There were times that I felt as though I should just quit and give up, and it was on those days I had to push myself further to have my family together again until we were complete.

Things weren't perfect in the way I wanted them to be, but they were still perfect in my eyes. We were just five months away from our closing on moving into our new home. If anyone knows how that process goes, they will understand me when I say a lot was going on during that time. Don't get me wrong I'm not complaining about it! I was ready for a new change and to move my family into a city where it was quieter. My experiences throughout the years, fighting for custody just showed me that everything that happens in life does not happen before its time.

I planned that morning just to be ready when Noah returned, we were all waiting at home together sitting around like kids in a candy store. As I sat there looking and waiting, I recall speaking to my daughters, all their excitement and their facial expressions were just priceless. My older daughter particularly knows how much of a fight I put up to get here, to finally be at a point where it was all calm and settled. She watched me each and every-day, at my highs and lows and especially on my worst days when I was drained and felt as though I wanted to give up. So, she couldn't help but smile in the end. The time was finally here now; and the waiting was over. When Noah walked into the house, we all hugged him and said, "welcome home!" He smiled as he hugged his sisters. His face looking like he won the whole world, with his cheek bones raised high showing off that big broad smile. I had no more tears, I couldn't cry anymore at this point even if I wanted to. All my tears just seem to vanish away, it was all smiles and butterflies. That feeling of feeling in love, when you know you have a tingle in the bottom of your lower abdominal area, the feeling when you know you are hungry but you're too excited to eat, the feeling of your chest when it tightens but its only because you're so overwhelmed with emotions, the feeling of sweaty arm pits when you're nervous but it's all excitement. The warmth that hits your body when you get a hot flash, but again its only because you are so overjoyed and filled with contentment. God had been good to me and my family. When I thought all was lost and I felt like giving up, He restored me in so many ways. If you don't have faith, then life doesn't feel right. It feels like you're just passing through. For me, faith gives me a purpose. Faith is where I find peace and learn more about myself.

The next day we woke up and it wasn't strange to have him in the house because we were still having visits with him while in care, but for some reason it felt a bit different. A good different to know that I would not have to return him to his father's residence or a stranger's home after being with his family. My wish was granted; and I had my son returned to me. From then on, we went about our days just like any other families would. There was no adjusting in that aspect, it felt like was just a piece of puzzle that was missing for too long that was finally found and returned.

As time went by, we embraced the fact that Noah was home and did things a bit differently going forward to ensure that he was feeling completely safe and comfortable. Everyday wasn't peaches and roses but we managed and got through each day with grace. I took each day one day at a time. I took my time to be patient with Noah, learning and getting to know him again. I helped his sisters to be patient with him. I knew all that had happened was profoundly traumatic for him, and he would require more of me than a normal child would. I also knew that I wanted to invest more in him to continue to ensure that he would keep on getting the treatments that he was already receiving with a therapist. A few months before Noah returned home, he was diagnosed with ADHD, ADD and ODD. This was not an easy pill for me to swallow, but I wanted to get to the bottom of his diagnosis. I never felt that he had any of these traits. I voiced my opinion on the diagnosis, and it was important for him as well to know. Even though Noah was diagnosed, he wasn't treated any different from his sisters nor did he get away with anything. I treated them all the same. Deep down I believed all along he was miss diagnosed. I could be wrong, but as a mother I was very keen with him and observed him over the years to know that much. Noah was bright and full of energy and life. That was a bit much for some to manage so when there is a child that does not seem to fit the mould, I find that we are quick to label. But I'll leave that for another chapter or another book. Each week and month there were new challenges faced. Some were easy and others I learned what to do as I was going along. Sometimes I remember wishing that kids could come with a manual. But then I thought that that wouldn't be much fun! Noah was still attending the school in the neighbourhood that he had been going to when he was in foster care. We were in the transition of planning around moving to a new school and closing things off with his current school. I can tell that he had already got used to his environment and the new friends that he had made. Even though it was hard again for us to move and change all that for each of the children, it was just as important for us to all have a new fresh start. It was bittersweet. Just a month before we moved, I took the kids to the house to pick out their rooms and to see the finished product. It had been a full 18 months of planning and talking about this house that they had seen in pictures. It was a reality now. When we drove up and parked our car on the driveway. All I could hear was "WHOAAAA! WOW! OMGS! Its so nice!" They were in disbelief that they were moving into such a beautiful house. They all jumped out the vehicle in such a rush and packed with excitement. This was a dream for them. Hearing about it and talking about it for so long they were anxious. The faces they had that day, I would not trade for anything in this world. I was very happy to move for my children and each step of the way that was all I had in mind.

As we entered the house, they were just busy everywhere I could hear chatters and echoes through out the house as they walked through. It was a great feeling, the same feeling that I had when Noah returned home the first day, it all came flooding back to me.

It was August 2015 when we moved into our new

home, the day came so sudden but for me it couldn't come quickly enough. I needed that new start, that I had been longing for so long for my children. After packing up with the movers all day from the house to storage, the drive on the way to the house seemed never ending for some reason. I can still hear them breathing as they slept in the back. The move had taken all day and it was night by the time we arrived. That still didn't stop their excitement. As I looked into my rear-view mirror, I can still see Noah's glossy eyes, trying to stay awake if possible. Ever so often I would hear "when are we going to get there? How much longer?" All I could say was "very soon!" We finally made it, everyone was awake and anxious to get into the new home and pick their rooms out, after going from room to room they made their final pick. Noah and I decided that his room would be next to my room. I remember making a joke about having him beside me, so that way I could monitor him if he sneaked out at night. They were all laughing. This night was one of the best feeling I've had in a while. So much to be grateful and thankful for. My children were happy and that was the most important thing. The following day we woke up and unpacked and sorted the boxes. They were very helpful as usual; they did not need any reminders to help unpack their rooms.

It was now a week into our new home, and they were all getting adjusted to our new environment, getting familiar with the park close by, the new neighbours and the malls. Noah enjoyed and liked the fact that he had a fresh start, he was excited about meeting new friends. We all needed a change. We had only moved in a few weeks before school reopened in September. Noah was previously attending public school in Toronto, so I decided seeing that we are embracing change, I wanted him and his sisters to learn more about religion in school. We decided that a Catholic school would be the best way to learn more about Christ while in a school setting. Noah was only in Grade 6 when he started in the Catholic school. At first, he couldn't understand why I decided to send him and his sisters to a Catholic school, but over time he learned how important it was for him and his family.

Noah had set out a list of things to accomplish and making new friends was one of the top five on his list. Before we moved, he would mention it at least twice daily, and so he did make those friends. Noah will get excited about the simplest things he was also happy about the school uniforms.

What I learned during this chapter:

Whenever there is darkness there is light. Pray for what your heart desires. I pray for months to get Noah back home living with us, because of that I believe my prayers were finally answered. When things don't work out one way, find another way to make it happen, don't give up no matter the circumstances at hand. In this chapter I also learned a lot about mental health and the resources that are available. When Noah was diagnosed as mentioned in this chapter, it was hard for me to accept it. The results were not that clear, I went into a place of blame, as a mother trying to put the pieces together: where you may have gone wrong, thinking and asking yourself questions, what did you eat during your pregnancy etc. I learned quickly to do my research and look at what symptoms each of the diagnoses would display and how common they were. Instead of staying at the stage of denial or misinformed, I recognised very quickly that he needed my support even more and most importantly my understanding. This was a big learning curve for my family but in the end, we were open and accepted the changes as they came.

CHAPTER EIGHT

Getting settled and comfortable in a
new environment, adapting to changing
things around for the positive.

WITH EVERY OTHER child, its never really a smooth transition when moving to a new area and having to start over again, but Noah was putting his best foot forward in making the process easier. His first experience in the school was when we enrolled his older sister for grade ten, we went to her high school to fill out all the paperwork. During the school visit, Noah had the pleasure of meeting the vice principal. It was a good first experience for him, he often talked about it over and over. He couldn't wait for his turn to attend high school and to join his older sister. The summer approached, and with all the busy planning for school and settling into our new home and neighbourhood, summer came and left us too quickly. I could not believe it was back to school time. I looked forward to the last two weeks of August each year: going into the stores with the kids, purchasing new school clothing and new back packs. They each liked the idea of starting fresh and new, especially Noah.

On the first day of school I would always take a photograph with my children before they each go their separate way. That morning was a rush in the house as usual, lining everyone up in their fresh new uniforms to take get a good photograph taken. All the planning and prepping was finally over, and it was time for them to start a new journey. I was happy for each of my children in a different way, knowing that this would be a new chapter for each of us and particularly for Noah. He had recently moved home permanently after so many years of constant custody battles. On the first day of school, dressed in his white-collar shirt and blue cargo pants, not to mention his fresh haircut he had just gotten a few day ago. He looked ready for the new changes and transition. Noah was finally going to experience what he had been talking about for the longest time, making new friends and having a blank clean slate and off to a fresh start. Off to school they went, Noah and his two younger sisters attended the same elementary school, each morning they would take the same bus together to and from school. As time went by, Noah was making friends, the school only had four hundred plus children, so this was easier for him as he transitioned. Noah had a keen sense for style and took great pride in his outward appearance. For some reason he would make his uniform trendy and loved a good pair of bright coloured running shoes. In fact, he had a pair of running shoes for every occasion, whether he was playing basketball or soccer or just going out. There was always a specific shoe that he would wear. I thought it was interesting at first and how could he be so interested in shoes. However, that was the least of my problems. I was always nervous for Noah, as he went through this transitional process in his life, or you can say a "mother's wor-ry" I was nervous and anxious about how the changes would affect him. I wanted him to know he was safe, and he didn't have to worry about living in another temporary house setting. He was going to be home permanently. I was nervous for different reasons. Noah was getting involved in school activities as they came up and whenever he had an opportunity. Over time, as Noah got familiarized with the school, he was known for being smart, a charmer, funny and a sweet talker. It wasn't always this way, there were times when Noah would get himself into trouble. He believed in making a change and always telling his story to help others. Noah would stand up for others when they were getting bullied and treated unfairly. Sometimes he would put himself in danger's way to help others, to the point where he would get caught and get himself into trouble. He was not an average child in my eyes. He would always think outside the box. He was the type of kid who has a big heart. When he did something wrong, he would be the first to admit it, even if he knew he will get his privileges taken away from him. Noah decided that he wanted to start working at an early age, he would always ask me what he can do between the ages of twelve to fourteen to make money. He was very ambitious. I had told him the only thing he could possibly do, that he would like, would be to deliver the local newspaper or learn how to mow the neighbour's grass and snow removal. It didn't take him long to have it all sorted out. Before getting him the details, Noah had a neighbourhood friend that he had made friends with within our new neighbourhood during the first couple of weeks of moving in. One day he went out with him and his friends' father, when he returned home, he had all the information for becoming a newspaper delivery boy. All the details were outlined for me. the only thing I had left to do was make the phone call for him to be signed up. Noah had taken it upon himself to ask the necessary questions and gathered the contact info for me to start the process. He was very persistent on getting this new job. It took roughly two weeks before he was working delivering the newspaper and flyers once a week after school. Whenever he wanted something there was no stopping him. His mind was already made up and ready to push through without a question. That was just one example of how determined he could be. He was reaping the benefits of working, and he was making one hundred dollars a month. The months were going great for Noah; we had our ups and down inside and outside of school, but he always ended up changing things to the positive in the end.

During the school year Noah would visit his father on the weekends. He was always looking forward to the visits after a long week at school. This was his getaway to unwind and reconnect with his father. Over the summer, he adjusted and made a lot of friends, this made me less worried about him returning to school. He was transitioning to his final senior year of middle school-Grade Eight. I was less worried about Noah returning to the school, during Grade Seven and over the summer, he adjusted and made a lot of friends. He was now transitioning to his final senior year of middle school - Grade Eight. Already familiar with the school and the new friends he had made the previous year. I could see the positive side to him, he appeared more confident and settled, all the hard work was paying off. He would brag about him being the "king" at his school and how the kids look up to him whether he was doing good or bad. Noah was more so happy about it being his last year and looked forward to joining his older sister in high school, as apparently, Grade Eight was an interesting year.

Noah was growing up in front of my eyes into a young man. His voice was deeper, he was growing taller than me and I could see the physical changes in him as the weeks and months passed us. For Grade Eight, Noah had set very high goals for himself and he wanted me to keep him accountable for them if he didn't follow through. For some reason he kept saying that his Grade Eight experience did not feel like school. The trips to his high school for Grade Nine, retreat and year end trip made it felt more like a vacation from school. I cherished the moments he had during this at school. It made things flow smoother for him in the end.

I can recall also prepping for graduation night. He wanted to dress in a way, wearing a white blazer with black dress pants. He looked all grown up on graduation day. It reminded me of his first birthday when he was dressed in a white tuxedo for his baptism. His Grade Eight graduation was a happy occasion and I was very pleased when he graduated, this was a big deal for him. Noah always had ideas in his head of what the day will look like for him and what he would be wearing form clothes down to the shoes and hair cut choice. On the day of graduation, the ceremony took place at one of the local high schools, the same high school that he would attend in the September of that year. As I sat in the auditorium waiting for his name to be called for his diploma, I felt the butterflies in my stomach while I sat there. My heart was overwhelmed and so proud of how much he had endured and how far he had come. It takes a lot for any child to go through such trauma and still push through. Noah had a fire that was in him. As I sat there waiting, I could not have been happier. Noah could see the smile on my face, he knew how much joy it brought me to see him graduate and the smile he brought to my heart; if it could have shown, it will be bright. He had made us so proud. Tears came to my eyes. The walk he had across the stage collecting his diploma was priceless. He had the walk of a King. Yes! Noah was proud of his accomplishments. He knew how far he had come and where he was going. That night was one of the best nights for my family to see him in a happy place. After the graduation ceremony he attended the reception at a banquet hall, where he continued to celebrate the rest of the night with his classmates. This was going to be Noah's favorite part of the night apart from receiving his diploma, you can only imagine the fun he had. Noah loved dancing, he talked about all the moves he was going to show off and how great he was as a dancer. Dancing was one thing he was confident about, he couldn't wait to leave the car; the doors of the car were open and shut so fast as he headed towards the front entrance of the reception hall to meet his friends.

At the end of the night we drove over to where the reception was held to pick him up, as we sat and waited in the parking area with the other parent before going into the building, kids were walking out shouting and singing leaving the parking lot, I can hear chatters how much fun they had and how they had wished the night would never end. As we sat there and continued to wait for Noah, I decided to make my way inside, I recall going into the building and waiting for him while he wrapped up the night talking and saying good-bye to his friends. I can tell he was disappointed to leave, he didn't want the night to be over, One of his friends came up to me and mentioned how Noah was a good dancer, Noah was exhausted at the end of it all, walking back to the car he talked about all the beautiful girls and how many of them he danced with. He was all smiles even though, from his eyes, you could tell that he wanted to sleep. His Grandmother was there to witness it all, I can tell she was also happy to see him accomplishing this milestone. I can hear all her praises and compliments she was giving to him and how happy he made her felt, he was always smiling no matter the circumstances, but that night was special for all of us. I hadn't seen him smile as much as this ever, so I could tell that this was one of his best nights of his life. I loved every bit of it, this is what I had wanted for him all along. I had wanted him to just be a kid and have the best days. It was a simple and easy wish, but it took a while for it to happen. I was in a happy place to see it. Sometimes, as mothers, we want a lot for our kids, and we do a lot for them to make them smile at the end of the day. It doesn't always happen on our time, but if you're persistent it will eventually happen. It took a while for me to see this in Noah, or maybe it was there all along, but he just needed that evening for me to see.

What I learned during this chapter:

During this part of my life I witnessed seeing my son as happy as he could ever be. His face gave me hope and a new meaning to life. I also learned to appreciate the simple things in life even if they're just a smile, a laugh or a memory. Throughout this chapter of my life, I realized how important it is to be patient and to have faith in everything that I was doing. With trial I knew that there would be errors, but without errors or failures I would not know half of the lessons I've learnt to date. You also need to have a strong and firm mind, when making decisions. I learned to celebrate with my loved ones each moment we got and to be happy for their smallest achievements. When my son graduated it was a big deal for both of us, I knew this was a milestone he wanted and looked forward to, leading up to his graduation I couldn't be more thrilled for him.

My advice is to celebrate the small wins; they're a gateway to the bigger ones.

CHAPTER NINE

High school junior year - Noah overcame challenges and obstacles throughout his first and second semester. Managing Suspensions and taking responsibility of his actions.

STARTING OUT GRADE Nine, high school, Noah couldn't have been happier to start another new journey in his life. Like he would always say: "a new and fresh start!" He loved the idea of starting new and having a blank clean slate. Noah was now attending the same school as his older sister. On the first day of school, Noah came home, and he had so much to say about his experience and first day of Grade Nine. He liked all the classes that he had selected earlier in the year, before ending Grade Eight. He talked about the new friends he had made and whom he was hanging out with during the lunch breaks, he also mentioned how nervous he was to eat his lunch on the first day in the cafeteria. As the week was coming to an end, Noah was very confident that this was one of the best weeks he had in a long time at school. As much as he was nervous about starting high school, he mentioned that he was over-thinking the idea and it was not like what you see in the movies. Noah had his own preconceptions, based on what he had seen in movies. However, that was not the case for Noah, and he was finding it much easier than he thought he would. Noah was worrying less about a lot of things. He took pride in his schoolwork. His homework assignments were getting done most of the time without me asking him to complete it, he also became more athletic very quickly and showed tremendous interest in other sports. He really enjoyed playing basketball with his friends after school at the local park and at the YMCA. Noah particularly loved playing with the senior guys, as it gave him an opportunity to show off his skills and to challenge his abilities. He knew he wasn't the greatest at it, but he did the best at playing the game. His natural love for it made it more fun for him. Noah would often talk about getting a scholarship after he had finished high school and making it to the NBA. He even went as far as writing it in his room closet on the wall that he will be playing in the NBA when he gets older. Basketball was on the top of his list.

There was a tryout in his school for basketball, I recall Noah trying out for the team. Leading up to the trials, he would come home and practice just to master his shots into the basket. When he realized that he hadn't made the team, it hurt every part of him. He came home that day and I could see that his heart was heavy. I sensed that something went wrong at school. As I sat there and watched the pain in his eyes as he told me he didn't make the team, it hurt me as well. He was shattered and broken from finding out the news. He couldn't understand why he didn't make it. As he sat at the dinner table, I could see heavy tears rolling down from his eyes. The only comfort I could give him were words of encouragement and remind him that he's smart and talented. Noah and I both knew that he did his best and that's all that mattered at the end of the day.

With Noah's personality he does not stay down for too long. After we had a good thirty minutes conversation about him not making the team, he was able to pull himself back together and think positive. I knew it wasn't an easy thing for him to do but he did it anyway. He wasn't going to let one decision get the best of him.

First semester report cards were coming home, and I couldn't be happier with his grades. He was pushing and excelling in every subject, I had no doubt and no worry that he wouldn't do well, each teacher had positive feedback to give about his grades. Everything was going perfectly for each of my children academically. I took Noah's advice and decided that I was going to join the local YMCA where Noah will play basketball with his friends. After many attempts of him telling me how much fun it would be, and that he will assist me in being my coach in the gym to help me get in shape, I realized quickly that this was his way of me getting him to the gym. Every other day he attended to play basketball with his friends. On my workout nights he would join me in the gym to play basketball, or workout with me while he waited for his friends to join him. Sometimes while working out, I could hear him from the track above that was overlooking the entire gym, shouting in excitement as he's enjoying his winnings. There was never a dull moment with him. I would always smile to myself and think how he got me to sign up for the gym and barely coached me at all. He was very smart at figuring things out to work to his benefit. When I asked him about it on our drive home, he would say to me: "you know what you're doing, in no time you will be in shape!" I couldn't get upset at him for using his brain on me, he was too smart, all I can do was smile and tell him how clever he was.

Semester One started out great for Noah but as we got to the middle and closer to the end of the semester, things started getting a bit rough for Noah. It wasn't all great days ahead. We experienced some high days and other we had our shares of lows. Some of those low days resulted in suspensions from school for a day or two here and there. I don't know of any child likes to be suspended, and Noah didn't like the feeling either. He was always concerned about his grades and how much his percentages would drop if he were not there to participate in assignments. Noah would always do his best not to have his grades drop. Grades weren't the only thing Noah was concerned about. During the middle of the semester, Noah experienced some bullying and a few racial hatred comments that were made from others around him at school. The students that were bullying Noah were friends of Noah's friends. There were times that he would ignore the comments and other times he would get upset about it; those days were very difficult for Noah and it dictated how his days and weeks would go during those incidents. He would always tell me about one student that would hang around one of his friends, this student would always call him a "nigger," or make him feel as though it was not ok to be black. His reaction to that was he would try and walk away, or he would stand up and voice his opinion on the matter. Noah always stood up for what he believed in even if he knew it was going to be a loosing battle in the end. That never stopped the student from bulling and calling Noah names, but it made him realize that he wasn't going to tolerate being disrespected. He stood up to the bully and was able to let him know that he was not afraid of him and his threats. Noah had a voice for himself and that was enough to have the bully back down. The bullying didn't stop right away but over time he noticed that he was not getting any attention and that Noah was not afraid of him. Over time we didn't hear any complaints from Noah about this student. Noah went on saying that he got the message clear. Noah was always told to be mindful of his friends and his surroundings, he was thought that the best way to deal with ignorance is to educate and give ignorant knowledge.

Before we knew it, exams came around, and first semester was over. Noah did well on his exams and managed to get through the difficulty. Going into second semester he was eager to start, as he was now going to be taking art of his favourite subjects and hobby. With his love for art that he developed over the months and years; he was ready to take his drawings to the next level. He started showing his interest in art from roughly the age of six years old. After I realized that he was drawing a lot and took his time with colouring, I knew he had a natural skill for drawing. Religion was also another class that Noah paid special interest in, he was always eager to know more about how men and women were created. Noah had lots of questions for the teachers and his father when it came to that class, he was never shy to ask about sex before marriage, he was curious to find out what is acceptable and not in God's eyes. He loved learning about the Bible and would always reference it to the way he was living his own life, especially the Ten Commandments.

Again, the months were going by quickly for semester two, all the extra curricular activities leading up to parent teachers meeting were here already, I kept thinking that this year was going by way faster than the other previous years. I was learning so much more about Noah during his first year of high school, as he was growing into a young teenager. Even though he started off the school year on a good note, made new friends and was enjoying his first year, he was experiencing a little of everything. In school he was meeting more new friends and acquaintances that he developed a relationship with over time. Some were good influences and others not so much. I was concerned about his decision making more time than others. When it came to the point of getting a suspension, those were the times when my heart would skip a beat for him. He had a group of friends that he would hang out with, which is when I started to see changes in his behaviour. I was now dealing with suspensions that were lasting three, four and five days. This wasn't Noah. It was hard for me to see that everything we had worked on was not getting practiced. Don't get me wrong, when Noah wanted to follow directions and be obedient, he would, but there was another part of him that sometimes would get peer pressured into doing things that neither him or myself would ever approve of. We were going through a rough patch again. However, I was always up for a challenge. Everything that I'd experienced before helped me in my current situation. Whenever Noah was experiencing a rough patch, I'd always look back to see how far we have made thus far and always kept a positive outlook that "this too shall pass." Noah had endured so much and had made a lot of positive steps in the right direction. So, I complained less and used each opportunity to see the good and work around it.

Noah was now on a ten-day suspension in second semester. I got a phone call from the school about him vaping in the bathroom. This was new for us, first to hear that he was interested in smoking and second he was on school premises. The suspension started in May of 2018. This was one of the longest suspensions he had ever received since attending school. During the suspension he was referred to an alternative program within the community. This program had other kids from different schools and grades, everyone was there for different reasons and worked at their own pace. He attended during school hours where he would complete his schoolwork. Noah hated attending the program but for some reason it grew on him during the

10 days. He knew he had more freedom doing what he wanted with the supervision, and he appreciated being able to do his schoolwork instead of falling behind. He didn't mind attending while suspended, there wasn't a lot of pressure throughout the day for him, he completed his work at his own pace. He attended daily for the duration of the suspension. Each morning a taxi would pick Noah up from home and he would take the local transit home or walk back on nicer days, if the weather allowed him to. Some of the days he would head straight to the YMCA where he would play basketball with his friends, or to the local Tim Hortons where his friends would congregate together over an icecap.

Noah was counting down the days left of his Grade Nine school year and was eager to work during the summer again. While he was attending the day program where he learned how to create a resume for himself, he wanted to start applying for jobs, a few weeks before school ended for summer break. He made the most of his time while in the day program. His plans seemed as though he had a backup. He talked a lot about having to work in his friend's pizza shop if no one else hired him. Noah was motivated by buying new clothes and staying current with fashion trends, so planning his summer to work was on the top of his list. Finally, the suspension was over, and Noah had prepared himself to return to school.

It was the weekend before Noah's suspension ended. He had visited his father that weekend in Toronto, as per usual I'll picked him up from the bus station on Sundays. I had just finished preparing for the busy week ahead with his sisters and for his return to school. Picking him up, he was wearing a new lilac cut off sleeve sweater and cargo shorts. I can see and smell the newness of it in the car. As usual we blasted the music and bopped to it on the highway driving back towards the house, this was a good and positive way to finish off his weekend; and besides he loved listening to music loud whenever the two of us were in the car. This was our special way of connecting and bonding with each other. Noah had been growing his hair for over a year but when we arrived back home, I noticed a huge change with his hair. He had received a hair cut while he was in Toronto that weekend, everything was taken down to one level. He looked sharp and ready for a change; the hair cut he received made him looked even more handsome. We rocked back and forth and sang along to songs until we got to the house that Sunday evening. He was reminded again that this was another fresh start for him going forward. As always, he acknowledged with a smile or let you know that he was aware and that he would do his best going forward. I was always confident and positive about how he was going to approach the week; he was already planning how different he would be going forward when he returned to school. The 10 day suspension made him realize how serious his actions were, he told me that a lot of his friends were doing it and he did not realize how serious it was until he was caught and confronted about it, he went as far as saying he got very defensive about it because he was embarrassed that I found out and the last thing he wanted to do was disappoint me. I knew it took a lot for him to say that to me, although I was not pleased about the 10-day suspension, I looked for the positive in all that was happening around him.

What I learned during this chapter:

I learned to be open and transparent with my children and more with myself, and by doing that I was able to see more of their personalities and help them through difficult times away from home. I also gained more insight into an average day at school for my children, what it's like walking in their shoes daily. They have struggles like adults do, be mindful not to dismiss their feelings and thought process. Take the time out to dig beneath the surface and help them in which ever way you can. When Noah told me the names he was called in school, it broke me. Each one of my children were called names at some point, this wasn't the first time I've experienced it with them. Pack your kids with knowledge and build them up to be sharp tools to stand up to the bullies. If we run away from our problems or teach them not to say anything, I believe we are silencing their voices and muting them, they are empowering the bullies to continue. Educate them how to stand tall in a positive way, there's only good rewards to come out of it. They will not only stand up for others but also themselves. It will allow them to build self esteem and character.

CHAPTER TEN

My worry as a parent when my teenage child does not return home from school.

Rewind to, May 28th we woke up at the same time as usual to get everyone ready for school. I made my way down the stairs to prepare my two younger children's lunches for school. While prepping, I could hear footsteps upstairs, everyone was up and moving around as expected. From downstairs, I could hear the shower running in the main bathroom that they used and chattering. I shouted from downstairs for my husband to get my youngest up and told him its time for her to wake up. Flipping pancakes, trying to make breakfast and pack lunches at the same time, I waited for my oldest to make her way down into the kitchen. I can hear the creak in her floor as she moves around in her bedroom. The floors always made this noise, and I knew exactly on what side of the room she was standing, depending on where the creaks came from. She finally made her way down after forty minutes of getting ready. I made my way up stairs to check on everyone else to ensure that they were also all on schedule. As I passed Noah's room to enter my room, I opened his door and noticed that he had just started rolling around slowly, attempting to wake making his way out of bed. I reminded him not to miss his taxi and that he should get something to eat without having to rush. That morning I also had to get into work early. After getting back to my room I went into the shower and prepared myself for work, I needed to get to the office by 8:30am and did not want to arrive late; at that time, we had one working car and I was relying on my husband to drive me to and from work. While I was getting ready, my older daughter was on her way out the house, I could hear her saying bye to her sister from where I stood at the top of the stairs, she called up to me afterwards telling me that she was leaving. I bent over from the top of the stair as I called back to her, saying her name and letting her know I would see her later. My husband had had the idea, that whenever we would leave each other, we should say "see you later," instead of "goodbye." My husband hated saying "goodbye," it was too final.

By this time, I was all dressed and ready for work, and as I was making my way back down the stairs, I noticed that Noah was almost ready, he had the bathroom to himself, so it didn't take him any time once he got into it. We all sat around in the kitchen as we ate our breakfast and watched the news, while waiting for my turn to leave the house. Noah's taxi had arrived at the door and as usual, the driver was beeping from the driveway. Noah quickly hurried to the door with his backpack in a scramble while putting his sneakers on. As usual, I told him to have a good day and that I'd see him later. I also reminded him that I would be home early and that he should make his way home, as school was finished. He then looked up at me and said: "Yes! I will be here." Within seconds he was out the door and into the taxi. I watched through my front glass doors as the taxi left the driveway.

My younger two daughters were also getting ready to go to the bus stop while I was heading through the front door and out to work. It was another sunny and bright day outside. On the drive into work my husband and I spoke about each of the kids and what we were proud of. With my oldest, we talked about how proud we were that she was coming to the end of her high school year and heading off to university. With Noah, we talked about how far he has come and how much of a bright future he has ahead of him. About our middle daughter, how grown-up she's getting and how responsible she is and with my youngest, we talked about her bright personality. There was something great about each of them and we were just so proud of all four of them. As usual, my husband would talk most of the time when he was driving me into work. We would always laugh, play music and take the time to act like little kids and each morning was different. When my husband dropped me off at work, I also told him that I'd see him later, when he returned to pick me up. I recall my day being busy at work that day, morning and afternoon. As soon as I knew it, my kids were home from school. I called home asking for them individually, this was to ensure that they were all at home safe and to also check on them each just in case they had experienced a rough day at school. When I called at 3.15pm my husband had answered the phone and mentioned to me that the three girls are home, but my son was not home yet. I wasn't happy with the news that he had not come straight home after his school. But I was pleased to know that the girls were home and that their day had gone well at school. My husband and I assumed that Noah must be out with his friends at the park, as it was not uncommon for him to go straight after school to hang out with his friends, so we weren't too worried. On my drive back to the house, I let my hair down out of my high bun, took off my shoes I had on and place my feet up on the dash board, the windows were open as the wind blew inside the car into my face. I felt so at ease, relaxed and happy that I was heading home after a long day. For some reason I felt the need just to be in the company with my children, nature was giving me messages that I just needed to relax and unwind when I entered the car. It wasn't a long drive home, and as soon as I entered the house my kids greeted me with hugs and kisses. I don't usually get the kisses but when I do, I appreciate it more. I was only disappointed that I wasn't greeted by my son; he would usually run down or slowly walk down the stairs saying "hello" to me with a squeeze on my shoulder or by him telling me how tired I look. On his happier days I did get hugs, and I appreciated him calling me "mama," there was a way he did it that put a smile on my face. I automatically asked his sisters if he had called or if they had seen him since they came home, they all answered no. His older sister mumbled and said, "you know how he is; he's always staying out late with his friends, he rarely comes straight home." I was very disappointed in his decision on staying out, especially after I had spoken to him on several occasions about returning home as soon as school was finished. I took out my cell phone and called his cell number, I was sent to the answering service. He had a MagicJack number that he would always call me from, and I would return calls on this same number when I was able to connect with him. I knew if he's around Wi-Fi wherever he was, he would have answered the phone or sent me a message. Right away I had my suspicions he was in a park somewhere with his friends. The time went on, dinner came and went, and he was still not home. At this point it was roughly about 8:45pm at night and after making numerous attempts on the phone trying to get in contact with him, I sat in the living room waiting for his arrival and was looking forward to hearing his reasons as to why he wasn't home earlier. I kept staring at the front door hoping that he would show up before it got too late. At about 9:00pm I heard the front doorbell ring. I knew right away it was him. As I walked toward the door to let him in, I could see his silhouette through the glass doors. Grateful and thankful that he made it home safely, I quickly hurried and open the door. Without a question he apologised quickly about being late and mentioned that he just wanted to hang out with his friends and lost track of time, not to mentioned he also had to walk twenty-five minutes to the house. My husband and I expressed our concerns and let him know that he could not return home this late again in the future. I could see how sorry he was about coming in late. The weekend prior to this incident happening on the school night Monday, Noah had spent the weekend in Toronto, it was a much bigger city compared to where we live, it is much easier to walk and get from point A to point B and public transit is easier to access as well. There are times when Noah acknowledges that he sometimes gets bored of not having much to do or doing the same things repeatedly, he enjoyed hanging out with his friends. This was very much the cause of him staying out late, whenever he visited Toronto, he returned home with the same mindset as though he was in the city, he was always Torontonian at heart.

What I learned during this chapter:

During this chapter of my life we all need to be gentle with ourselves, take time out to rest and relax when needed. Be present with your children and loved ones even on their worst days.

Noah's Christening and 1st Birthday in Toronto, ON

Noah at 8 months in Toronto ON,
at his Grandmothers house with his favourite teddy.

Noah and his mother at 9 months in Toronto ON
in his Grandmothers living room

Grade 8 grad photo June of 2017
and collage of some of his friends

This is the last photo that was taken of Noah in May 2018

CHAPTER ELEVEN

Continuation of Chapter One - Fast forward to 15 years later.

May 29th. 2018

WE CONTINUED AND drove home, after a long day at work. My other three daughters were home, it was an average evening again and it was good to be home at such an early time. I loved days like these when I was able to come home, make dinner and be present with the family. I was expecting Noah to walk through the door any minute for dinner, as we had spoken the previous night about him coming home late, so I was expecting him earlier than the day before. At this point I had already finish preparing dinner and was relaxed. Once again, Noah did not come home for dinner. As the times passes, and with every minute and hour that went by, I kept looking at the clock and at the front door, expecting him to walk through it. No sign of him. I was informed that he did not call or return home that day after school was finished. As the time passed, I kept opening the front door thinking that he should be walking down the street as I looked outside. I also had thoughts and suspicion that he was going to call me to ask me to pick him up from one of his friend's house. It was not that unusual for him to hang out after school and stay out with his friends, but it was more worrying as the time passed without me having any knowledge of where he would be. I trusted him when he said he was going to be home earlier the next day. 8:30pm passed - 9:30pm passed. As the time passed and crept up on me, I went outside and sat down on my neighbour's front porch awaiting his arrival home. While we were there, I kept looking up and down the street as the darkness set in. The neighbour, myself and my husband talked for a while as we waited for Noah return home. I recall sitting on a cement surface directly facing their front door when a little baby bird fell from its mothers nest unto the hood of my neighbour's car, which was parked on her driveway, for some reason the bird managed to get stuck under the hood of the car. We all tried frantically to rescue the bird, as we attempted to open the hood of the car, for some reason, the hood would not open for at least five minutes. Eventually we managed to open the hood, and we realized that because of where the bird was sitting, if we opened the hood any further his or her wings could potentially be clipped, so slowly we shifted open the hood while moving the bird forward out of the way. Finally, we managed to get the little bird out. The bird appeared to be ok and not injured, but we couldn't return the bird back to its mother's nest, and the bird was too young to fly back up. The bird was now placed in the garden in front of the house so that his/her mother could find her in the morning, when looking for food. My neighbour had mentioned that the birds had built a nest in the peak of her house and we thought that it may have fallen from there. We were all puzzled about how the bird ended up in the crease of the hood, after it had fallen from the nest. The moral of the bird story is that as humans we were all born to be nurturing individuals in some way shape or form. I immediately thought about Noah and how far we have come and the journey ahead of us. I knew that night at that moment of rescuing that little bird that Noah was going to be ok. I was proud of him and the changes that he had made for himself. I knew that he had my support 100% just like how the bird was rescued; it dawned on me that I would be Noah's Rescue.

Right after the rescue of the bird, we headed in for the night, but there was still no sign of Noah. As I walked toward my front door, I took one last glance down the street that we lived on looking up and down to see if I could see him walking towards the house, but there was no sign of him. As I closed my door, my anxiety started to set in on me like a child waiting for a roller coaster ride at Wonderland. Butterflies filled my stomach, a tremendous anxious feeling and worry came over me, at this point I was clueless as to why he didn't call or come home for dinner. As we continued to prepare for the next work and school day, I checked social media and saw that he had still been active online throughout the evening.

I continued to settle down for the night, and I managed to take a shower to relax my nerves while waiting for my son to get home. Before I went into the shower, I asked my husband to stay downstairs in the living room and wait for him to get home. I was so overwhelmed by the thought of not knowing where he was that I fell into a deep sleep after getting out the shower and searching online to see when the last time he was active online.

I woke up suddenly from a deep sleep on the morning of May 30th, 2018 at roughly about 12:15 A.M. in the morning. Immediately I came out of my room and investigated his room and noticed he was not there. His bed was still made up perfect and his curtains were still pulled to the one side just the way he had left it the morning on May 29th, 2018 before leaving for school. On May 30th roughly at 12:30am my husband was still downstairs when I yelled out his name asking if Noah was there in the kitchen. He replied to me and told me that Noah hadn't returned, nor had he called. We both thought it was weird and not in his character not to return home on a school night. After giving it, some thought, that he wasn't home, we decided that we would call the local Police to report him missing. I was dressed at this point ready to go searching for him. If he was at one of his friends' house or the local coffee shop, I knew the police would be able to help me locate him much quicker. I needed to know at this point he was found and safe. I recall one of the last messages I sent to him was if he doesn't return my calls or text, the Police would be called. As I called the Police, my heart skipped a beat. After getting off the phone and as I waited for the Police to arrive; I gathered his friends' names and contact information, as I thought there might have been a chance that Noah would have been at one of their homes. I also provided a photograph of Noah for them to make it easier to identify him. As I sat there waiting, my heart was beating at a rapid speed, my palms were sweaty, and my armpits felt damp. The worrying and the anxiety I had before falling asleep was worse now after waking up and knowing that he still wasn't home. I messaged Noah's phone and called numerous times, but there was still no answer; his phone would ring out before going to the answering service, leaving us to listen to his voice recorded message. The Police officer was now at my house at this point to take our statements, she also called Noah a few times while she gathered all her information on his possible whereabouts. I made another call to his phone and I was left with his voice again requesting to leave a message. The officer assured us that they would send out other officers to search the area and assured us that he would be found and returned home. We were also told to notify them if he didn't show up to school the next day, its important to let them know right away, and they would proceed further. We waited up the rest of the early morning expecting his return home, hoping and praying that my phone would ring or the officer that came to my house would return back with Noah. I went to sleep roughly at 4:30 am that morning after my eyes struggled to stay open. I was awake again at 6:30am, Sick with worry, I called Noah's phone, once again with no answer. I went into his room and stood by the window asking out loud: "Where are you Noah? Why didn't you come home? Are you hurt?" My husband told me they would find him and that I should try and relax and not think the worst. It was time to wake up the rest of my children to get them ready for school. When his sisters woke up, they each asked for him and if he came home, they suspected and seen how worried I was, I also assured them that the police were called, and they are going to help us locate where he is. I suggested to my older daughter to look around at school to see if he may have gone to school, and to also notify us whether he's there or not. I got myself ready for work after everyone was off to school. Throughout the morning I was anxious heading into work, I wanted school to be open to find out from Noah why he didn't come home the night before. I wanted to speak to him to find out if he were upset, I just wanted to hear his voice telling me that he fell asleep at a friend's house and he's sorry and that it won't happen again. I prayed for him that he was in a safe place. Still thinking positive, with my fingers crossed. We all went about our day, my kids each headed for the school bus as I make my way into work that morning, feeling tired and exhausted from lack of sleep and overwhelmed with anxiousness. I also asked my husband to call the school as well to see if he was there while I was at work. That morning, when we contacted the school, we were informed that they would notify us if he showed up that morning.

While I was at work that morning, I kept my phone on waiting anxiously for a phone call from home, school and the police. It was 9:00AM and I was still waiting to get a phone call. I called home and asked my husband if the school or his older sister had confirmed that he was there. He said to me that the school confirmed that he didn't show up and his sister couldn't find him either. We notified the police immediately and let them know as requested. I recall calling Noah's phone through out the morning leaving messages after messages without a call back. At this point my thoughts were he's most likely at a friend's house skipping school for the day or half a day, maybe he was drinking and he's out drunk still asleep, I had wild thoughts that will linger ever so often when my anxiety took over. Throughout the day our eldest daughter confirmed that his friends attended school that day. I just prayed that he was well and that he was just being a teenager. At this point I was beyond nervous and worried about him, after not seeing him since the day before he left for school. I was so worried about where he had slept, what he had for dinner, who he was with and what could have upset him to the point where he didn't come home on a school night. That morning I was assigned to be out of office in the field doing inspections, but I decided to stay in the office, so that I could be accessible by the phone.

What I learned during this chapter:

During this chapter of my life, I learned being persistent you will get the answers you need, whether good or bad. Life will always have its ups and downs. Staying focus no matter the circumstances. This chapter of my life also was a time when my faith and strength was tested, I wanted to give up so many times, but my inner spirit would not allow me to. During Noah's first high school year he was exposed to much more than what he could have anticipated, the pressure, bullying and fitting into a new school. His love for making new friends helped him along the way and his openness about life and how far he came helped him. It was also during this time, Noah would always say to me when he gets older, he wants to write a book, because he has so much to say. When your child does not return home from school it's not a pleasant experience any parent should go through, my anxiety level was out of control and it almost got the best of me. I had to practice a lot of breathing techniques to help me manage from having a panic attack, its not as easy as it sounds, but the one thing that kept me together was knowing that my family need me more at this point than before. It was the last thing that needed to get added to what we were experiencing already

CHAPTER TWELVE

The search for Noah within the community by family, friends and strangers turns out to be my family's worst nightmare.

THE LOCAL POLICE were now canvassing the area searching for him after being notified that he did not show up for school that morning. My family and his father were notified that he had gone to school the day before and he didn't return home. No family member had heard from Noah nor had they seen him, when he was out with his friends, he would typically call his father, if he doesn't update me on his whereabouts he would answer his fathers phone call or return his calls without hesitation. That day he refused to answer and there were no return calls even after his father had reached out to him.

It had been twenty-four hours since he went missing

and didn't return home from school, with no telephone calls and no form of connection with him. Searches were taking places everywhere within the community; in the mall, the movie theatre, coffee shops and all fast food places. Wherever there was a possibility, it was searched. At this point my emotions and my patience were running low. It didn't matter what had happened during the day and whatever the reason was why he didn't return home, all I wanted was to be able to hear his voice and for him to tell me was safe with his friends.

I tried to stay concentrated on my tasks at work and to think positive, I distracted myself and kept extremely busy and just focussed on finding him. I was terrified of the unknown. The local police attended his school and were given confirmation from some of his friends that he was last seen the day before on May 29th, they had told the police he was by the local canal, swimming with other friends. I was at work when my husband called me and told me the information from the Police on where Noah was last seen the day before, he also informed me that they had searched our home as part of the search for him as well. Hours had gone by and the community, friends and family were all aware that he was missing at this point. The searches continued for him. At this point it was after 1:00PM that day, I was told by my husband and a detective, that was now working the case, that they would search the water canal area. I wanted everywhere to be searched and knew that it was great that they were actively trying to find him. Throughout the day they continued to search, and the day was coming close to an end for me at work, when I received another phone call from the detective informing me that the water area is still getting searched to see if there is a possibility of him being there, seeing that he was reported last seen at the canal the day before. I was also asked if I would be ok with them using the photo, I had given them to put on the media for an Amber Alert. This was all becoming and feeling like a nightmare, it was terrifying to know that they were searching the water and the thought of his photograph would be plastered over the media as a "missing child." I've seen so many movies and shows and it dawned on me what I had seen in a show called "the next 48hrs" was now happening to me. It didn't feel real and it didn't feel right. As it got later and later by the hour, I could feel my body becoming more and more tense and the feeling of becoming physically and mentally paralyzed with the thought of not knowing where he was or if he was safe. My heart was beating a thousand miles per hour and I could hear it every beat it gave, it gave with a heavy thump and my mouth was becoming dry, my saliva seemed as though it was drying up quickly in my mouth. My thought at this point was "why are they wasting time searching there?" They should be finding out where his friends live and going to their homes. Feeling hopeless and clueless, I trusted that they were carrying out their duties the way they should be done. After getting off the phone with the detective, I recall informing my supervisor at the time briefly what I was dealing with through out the day and that I had not had any contact with Noah. We would speak occasionally about our children and we both had a positive outlook that he would return home, when she heard the news. She was confident that he would return home with the perfect excuse and that maybe this was a stunt to get my attention. We both chuckled about it at that time.

It was now 4.30PM, it was the end of the working day and my husband was coming to pick me up. He had dropped me off that morning, I was relieved to leave work after hearing about everything all day, while not being physically at home. On the drive home, it was intense and overwhelming. Still feeling hopeless, tired and confused as to why we cannot locate Noah, I told my husband we are going to find Noah before it gets too late and before it gets dark again. I recall telling him that I was not going to sleep tonight until he's found. I could not sleep with the fact that he was out there and us not knowing where he was another night. My husband informed me that the officers and dive team were still out by the water searching for him. We planned on the drive home that I would change my uniform and we would visit the canal. I couldn't get there fast enough, the ride home seemed as though it was the longest ride. I wanted to see everything that was being done and to get as many more details as possible. I just wanted to see the officers and the detectives face to face and for the search to end, with Noah calling one of our phones or showing up at the house. We had driven past the canal where the officers were conducting the search, and we quickly drove by when I saw two police marked vehicles, one was a car and the other an SUV type vehicle. There was also a vehicle that was shaped like an armoured truck, I couldn't really make out what was written on it, but I knew it was the search and dive team. The surrounding area was cautioned off with yellow tape, the kind that you would will typically see at a crime scene or whenever there is evidence that needs to be protected. I've watched a lot of movies and studied in this field and I knew that something did not add up.

I was confused at this point, it was now 5:00PM and it wasn't clear to me why they were still at the canal area looking for him. We drove past the canal and got home to change out of my work uniform and to make sure my other kids were safe and ok. As soon as I entered the house, my other kids were so confused and appeared to be in panic mode, concerned for their brother and his safety. I assured them that everyone was out looking for Noah and that the police were doing their jobs. My middle and oldest daughters had said to me that earlier during the day, while they were at school, they were getting messages and receiving screen shots from friends and strangers indicating their brother "drowned," there were also messages stating he that he had "committed suicide." There were numerous screen shots that were sent to them of messages from his friends who were last seen with him. It was beyond stressful and overwhelming. At this point, I asked them not to go on social media and not to respond to any of the messages that were sent. I assured them that I was going to find Noah today and we would not go to sleep until we know where he is or that he has returned home. My middle daughter was crying, her tears flow down her face heavily and distraught by the messages she had received earlier that day. I changed my uniform shirt quickly then headed back out to the canal area to help with the search of Noah. When I drove past the canal again, I begged and prayed to God not to let Noah be here. My palms were sweaty, and my heart was still beating from the anxiety rush that I was having all day. As I approached the canal there was a female officer sitting in an SUV that was parked on the grass, with the vehicle facing towards the road. I observed a male wearing what appeared to be a diving suit type clothing, close to the canal bank, it appeared to me that there was another diver in the water. The male that was on the canal bank close to me appeared as though he was wearing a black diving suit and had an instrument in his hand facing the water, he kept looking at the instrument as he was walking along the banks of the canal. I stood there watching every move they made and was still confused as to why they were still there searching. The yellow tape was blocking off the perimeters of the bank stopping close to the paved walkway. The female officer that was sitting inside the SUV was looking at her computer screen and the surrounding areas. She looked over at us and made eye contact, while we stood there for a few minutes in silence looking on. It was shocking to just stand there, not knowing where I should start my search and how I was going to go about it. My husband and I decided that we should speak to the female officer sitting in the SUV. As we approached that black SUV from the passenger side, she rolled the windows down and she asked if she could help us. I recall identifying myself as Noah's mother. We asked her what was the update on the search, and why were the officers out here still searching by the water of the canal bank? The officer informed us that Noah's friends at school said he was last seen swimming around the canal between 6:00PM-6:30PM and that they are ruling out the possibility of him being in the water. We also asked the officer if any clues were found or any pieces of clothing by the canal? She told us that there were three pieces of clothing that were found and that we could go to the police station and possibly identify to see whether the clothes belonged to Noah. She couldn't give us any new details about the search but informed us to go and speak to the detective that was leading the case and to see the clothing. At this point, we decided to head over to the police station to speak to the detective and see if the clothes that were found was in fact Noah's. The station was only a two minutes drive away from where the canal is. We arrived in the parking lot and I thought to myself I cannot stand being here. One reason I felt that way was because I had been in a car accident a month before outside my work and I had to attend the same police station to make a report. Here I was again walking into the station to identify clothing that had been found. My stomach was in knots at this point from anxiety and hunger, as I hadn't eaten that day and had just had a little to drink here and there. We were in the waiting area and I could hear my stomach making noises both from being nervous and having full blown anxiety. As I sat there and waited, I couldn't keep still, my legs were shaking and again my palms were sweaty, I could feel the sweat dripping from my armpits. There were a few people I noticed coming in and out, I could hear the sound and noise in the room as it got difficult to hear, it sounded muffled. It felt as though I was this little tiny person inside a huge room, and the feeling of being under a microscope. Suddenly I heard the door inside the police station opened, I looked up at and there was a man wearing a blue light-coloured shirt, dark blue patterned blazer with a darker shade pants. He walked towards us and introduced himself to us as the detective that is working the file. At this point he had asked us to come into a room in the back and have a seat. Everything from this point seemed as though it were in slow motion, it felt like I was in a movie that I had watched before and, I wanted to fast-forward to the scene where there was a happy ending. As we sat down the detective was asking us questions about Noah and his personality, health, family and friends. They were just general questions, nothing out of the ordinary I thought. The detective updated us on his team of officers, he informed us where they searched including all the places we suggested. He also informed us that the search and dive rescue team was also still searching the waterway, to rule out the possibility of him being there also. A lot of searches had taken places throughout the day with no result in finding him. We asked about the clothing that was found by the canal and the detective confirmed they did find a shirt and a pair of socks on the canal bank. We wanted to see if it was Noah's shirt and socks and requested to see it. The detective brought in a brown envelope in his hands. He was also carrying a black pair of gloves. The envelope was placed on the table in front of us. After requesting to identify the clothing the detective slowly put on the black gloves and opened the seal of the brown envelope. The detective placed a black shirt and a pair of black Nike ankle socks onto the table in front of us. I wasn't allowed to touch it, however when I saw the socks, I knew right away that they were Noah's ankle socks; there was something about the location of the Nike sign that I remembered and I knew that I had washed those same socks the weekend before. The black shirt was a t-shirt with a crew neck. The shirt wasn't as easy to identify as the socks, but I knew it was his, due to the size and the way the sleeves looked. Noah loved wearing black and it was a new trend for him wearing plain black shirts. I was very confused at this point as to why would he leave his clothing outside for someone to steal it. Why didn't he just pack it up when he left? Knowing him, he would always have had extra clothing in his backpack, I figured he must have accidentally forgot it and left it behind on the canal bank by accident. We were able to inform the detective that it was his clothing; but at this point my husband and I were still not sure why his clothes would be left. As we sat there, trying to think of a reason why Noah may have left his clothes, I informed the detective that this was not like him, we knew him too well to even think of him doing such a thing. It was roughly between 6:10PM and 6:30PM and we were still sitting there, trying to figure out a reason for the clothing to be left behind and Noah's whereabouts. Suddenly, there was a knock on the door. It was one of the front desk staff we had spoken to when we arrived at the station. She had with her a piece of paper which she handed to the detective and whispered to him in a low voice. I didn't hear what she had said to him, however he asked to be excused from the room as he had a very important call he needed to take. When the detective left the room, I mentioned to my husband what could be more important for him to leave the room while discussing a missing child? I figured that this was just a regular thing that they do, while in the middle of a case or maybe he was the only investigator that was on shift. We sat in the room waiting for the detective to finish on the call thinking of where Noah could possibly be. Silence filled the room while we waited. I could hear the clock ticking loudly. As I stared through the window, I could see cars going by, life just seem to go on for everyone else while I sat there in distress and worry. I was finding it very hard to keep still in my chair, I found myself fiddling trying to keep my composure and to remain focussed on where Noah could possibly be. With every breath I took it got heavier and harder for me to breath, twenty-four hours had gone by without us seeing or hearing from him; no contact by phone, text or social media. No return calls, just an answering machine whenever we would call his phone number. Everyone in my family was calling; they were calling his sisters as well, who were still at home, waiting for Noah, just in case he showed up. His sisters were also told if he does return to call us immediately.

Five to ten minutes had already gone by since the detective left the room. We were sitting in an area where there was a glass wall where you can look out into the station and see the main area and lobby. I could see the detective walking back towards the room where we waited. As he entered the room, he closed the door behind him and walked towards us. I could hear his shoes making a knocking sound on the cement floor with every step he was taking. I recall looking over at my husband and he had the coldest blank look on his face. I looked back at the detective as he sat down in front of us, he slowly placed his hands on the table with his palms closed and hands crossing over each other; the look that was on his face was a look that I have never seen before. His eyes looked as though he was starting into my soul and my core. We all sat in a moment of silence that seemed like minutes. Suddenly the detective said: "Natalie, I am sorry to tell you that they have found Noah." I didn't know exactly what he meant when he said "sorry," but I did know that if it had been good news then he would not have said "sorry." Immediately, I didn't want to hear what else he had to say to us, I remember screaming and saying: "No, its not true, why are you lying to me?!" I continued to sit as he told me what had happened. He told us that they had found Noah's body at the bottom of the canal and he had drowned. The pain that I felt within the depth of me felt as though someone had run me over with a tractor or a train. Everything around me felt numb and silent, my soul and spirit left my body immediately when I heard what had happened. The cry that I gave out was a cry that when I cried out, I couldn't catch my breath. My heart felt as though it had stopped beating. I got up from my seat and recall pacing back and forth from one end of the room to another, holding my head. I wanted to rip every fibre out of my hair. I was in total shock and disbelief and could not grasp the news I just received. My husband, I can hear his voice shiver as he's talking to me, telling me: "it cannot be true." My tears flow as they wash my face, I ask my husband to ask the detective if he can go and double check to make sure that its him, because I didn't believe what he was saying to me now. I wanted to make sure that the photograph that was given to them during the search, was the same person they had found. I recall the detective saying, "I can double-check for you." As he exits the room, I kept asking my husband: "why are they lying to me? Please tell them to stop;" and "it wasn't true." It did not take much time before the detective returned to the room with the same face he had had before and the same news. The detective confirmed that it was in fact Noah. At this point, my life turned upside down, I felt as though my spirit had left my body and all that I had was gone. All I heard was the quiet and the still of the room. I could feel my heart beating on thee tip of my tongue, my saliva dried up instantly in my mouth leaving it feeling as though you're going to faint. This was an end to my physical relationship and connection with Noah.

During this chapter leading up to finding out my son had passed away, was beyond difficult and extremely hard finding out the news. As a any parent you hope and pray for the best, this was my attitude leading up to the horrible news. It was a shock for me after as you can only imagine, not that it made it any easier hearing the news, but I thank God for having my husband beside me when

I found out. The simple thought of having him there to help me process my thoughts and to physically be there was important looking back. We don't have to be alone during difficult and trial times, if someone wants to be there for you in which ever way, they can support, allow them to be.

CHAPTER THIRTEEN

Healing from being broken hearted, in everyway. I learnt that the only person you can rely on is God and yourself.

IT WAS THE most heart wrenching time for my family, when Noah's sisters, brothers and extended family and friends heard the news they were in shock and in disbelief just like everyone else, they couldn't understand how this could have happened to us. I recall hugging my children so tight as though I was going to lose them also. The tears that were falling from their eyes felt as though they were heavy and cold as they rolled down their cheeks. I did not want to let them go. I feared the minute I did, I was going to lose them also. As I sat down on my chair in my living room surrounded by everyone, I could hear the noise, everything appeared loud as though the world was closing in on me. I felt the world on my shoulders, with every whisper, I heard the voices sounding heavy in the room. I prayed that the horrible bad dream would end and that everyone would disappear when I opened my eyes. I recall the doorbell ringing late the first night and as soon as I heard it, I jumped up, thinking that Noah was at the door. I didn't tell anyone or my husband what I was thinking. I opened the door with my husband, and it was Noah's teachers along with the principal and vice principal at the door. My body was there physically but my spirit and my mind were elsewhere. I stood in front the door feeling lightheaded from not eating for the last twenty-four hours, I was lost for words and thoughts; as pain and grief settled in slowly. I couldn't even recall what my kids said after they heard the news. It was just a big blur for the first week, and it was hard to retain anything throughout each day I wake. Not that it got any clearer after that, it was very difficult not being able to shut my eyes because I was fearing having some sort of nightmares or was terrified that if I fell asleep, I wouldn't know when Noah arrived home. Without having any sleep at nights, I could still feel the heaviness as I lay in bed. The feeling of being unsettled and unsure as to what is really happening. My thoughts were scrambled as though I am watching television and I had turned to a channel that looks like little black and white dots clustered in front of the television. Each morning I would wake up and wish the day would be over with. I didn't have the energy and the will to wake up and get out of my bed, but I pushed myself whenever I saw my other children. I knew that they needed me at this point more than anything else in the world. Feeling lost for words and thoughts while my days would come and go. With the detective still working on the case, I was eager to know what had taken place by the canal which caused my son to lose his life. I waited a few days for the autopsy to be completed, when the results came back, we were notified by the coroners stating that there was no sign of trauma to his body, there was nothing on the report that could have led us to a conclusion as to what had taken place. I was beyond disappointed and relieved at the same time. I was relieved to know that no one had hurt my baby and was disappointed that they would not find any other clue as to how he could have drowned.

During the investigations a lot of teenagers were interviewed, some of whom were Noah's friends. Everyone who was interviewed did not arouse suspicion and their stories all checked out according to the detectives working on the case. During the investigation there was a lot of social media attention to the case. I was committed to and invested in finding out the truth and discovering exactly what happened by the canal that day. While the case being investigated, I couldn't bear the thought to sit at home, it did not settle well with me not doing or saying anything. I felt hopeless that Noah had gone swimming with six to nine of his friends and no one had seen or heard what had happened to him. After I fell asleep in Noah's room one night, I woke up with a plan to make a video to the public, a video that was going to ask if anyone knows what happened, to come forward. I wasn't going to accept that no one knew or did not see what happened that day. The message that I intended to project in the video was that I would not stop until I knew what had really happened to my son. Desperate searching, digging and looking for answers; answers that I knew I would most likely will never get. I can recall while making the video, I was barely able to put a sentence together, my jaws were clenched tight. I couldn't open my mouth to form my words or to say a full sentence correctly, the feelings of anger, hurt, confusion and the feelings of betrayal and pain had settled in quickly. I had never felt this low or been to such a cold place like this in my life before. Everything that I experienced felt as though it was a terrible nightmare movie I was watching. I never imagined that I would have been in a position like this. I just gave birth to my baby boy "yesterday," and he was taken away from me today. All these thoughts filled my mind and settled with me for quite some time. "Why was this happening to me?" I couldn't believe, understand or wrap my head around the fact that this was real. It was an experience that I kept telling myself was a bad dream and that I would soon wake up.

Many of my questions continued to go unanswered. My son's belongings had gone missing from the canal when he went swimming. He had left his grey and green new pair of running shoes and a rose gold apple cell phone on the canal bank, while he swam in the water that day with his friends. Prior to going swimming, he attended a close female friend's house where he changed out of his school uniform into regular clothing before heading to the canal with those friends. His backpack was left back at that friend's house for him to retrieve after they had finished swimming. Suspicious messages were also left that day on social media regarding him being missing. I questioned it, but nothing came out of it. Everything seemed in a daze right after I heard the news, it was hard for me to make sense from the stories that were given to me. Family, friends, the neighbours and the community were very supportive. I recall my house being full everyday. Everyone that my family knew were so supportive with dropping by flowers and delivering cards, offering a helping hand and even meals. I did feel overwhelmed by all the support; however, it is what I needed during that time. Prayer was my best source of comfort at this point. There was nothing that anyone could have given me or could have said that would take the feeling away. As my family, near and far, heard the news, they all gathered and supported me along the way. My aunt, that I grew up with as a child, came to support my family. She stayed with us and if it weren't for prayers and her, I would not be able to write and share my story today. She came in and really took charge, there were mornings that I didn't feel like taking a shower and she would remind me to go and ensure that I washed and combed my hair. She helped me to do even the simple things such as eating. I had forgotten to eat due to lack of appetite. I lost roughly ten pounds within less than two weeks. My aunt was there ensuring that I eat, she forced me to eat my first meal which was toast and a cup of mint tea. This was painful for me, as I bit every piece of my toast, my mind wondered away as I thought of Noah and if he had anything to eat; and I also reminded myself that I was waiting for him that day to have dinner, when he never came home. I couldn't help my thoughts. I continued throughout my days feeling as though I was weightless and floating in space. My mind continued to wonder

After two weeks of planning for Noah's burial, the day was here for our first viewing. I had to face everything head on.

As I walked into the front doors to enter the building, I couldn't see into the room clearly at this point where his casket was place. We were greeted by the director and staff and then escorted into the room before everyone else arrived. I stood outside the room shaking and shivering as though it was a cold winter day. I wasn't prepared to go in however I knew I had to. I wanted to see Noah, I wanted to see my baby, I hadn't seen him since he left for school that morning of May 28th. As the director opened the door to the room where Noah rested, my stomach felt weak and I felt as though I wanted to vomit. My other children walked in with me, as we make our way to the front of the room it was one of the longest walks I've ever taken. I was hoping and praying for the last two weeks leading up to this day, that I would walk into the room and it would not be him lying there; my reality settled and dawned on me as I take those steps at our viewing. In shock and disbelief that it was my baby there, my world was torn apart again, this was another reality I had to face, Seeing him there, I could hear the detective's voice again in my head, when I received the news on that first day. It was another day I wanted to just be done and over with. The feeling of getting numb was setting in and was becoming too familiar at this point.

The following day was the funeral and burial service. I remember waking up that morning early, after barely sleeping the night before. I sat on the edge on my bed in my towel as the sun came up and peeked its way into my sheer curtains. I gazed outside, watching as the sun peeked through my window curtains, reflecting on the years we have had with Noah. Not sure how I was going to get through the day, I wanted it to be over with before it even started. I managed to write Noah a letter that morning. Before I could even finish a sentence, I kept tearing the paper out of the book, what was I going to say to him? Where do I even start? The palms of my hands sweaty, my heart was pounding as I tried to put my sentences together. There wasn't anything that I could say to him that will make it right; if words had a way of bringing back the dead, I would forever write to him begging him to please return. So, I started my letter after several attempts trying to perfect it for him. I called it "my love letter to Noah." I wanted him to know how I felt about him and how much I loved him. I knew I wouldn't have enough time to read it and was not sure if I would have the strength to read it out loud.

That morning when everyone else woke up it was one of the quietest mornings in the house since we heard the news, I can feel that pain and the tenseness within the air. Sad faces of pain and sorrow. I felt the pain for my other children, this was the first funeral that they had experienced in their lives and the thought that they would always have that memory of their only brother's funeral was especially hard for me. I recall as a child going to funerals with my grandmother and that experience alone was always painful and difficult for me, whether it was a family member or not. As a child, the thought of the experience drained me mentally for a long time. It pained me more to know that this was the first experience of death for my children. As a mother I always try to protect them from all the bad and the evil; but this one was out of my control. I was left with no explanation as to how I was going to help them heal or simply just to help them get through their days, months, and years ahead.

After travelling to the funeral home, driving for over an hour into the west end of the city, I was lost in thoughts, my mind wandered far and long praying that I was going to wake up from the nightmare again. On the way down, I was getting lots of messages on social media from his friends that couldn't make it. I could feel my phone vibrating into my sweaty palms. I opened my phone to my Facebook app, and I recall reading a message from someone who had added me as a friend during the first two weeks after Noah's passing. I didn't know this young man, but his online caption that morning sparked my attention. This young man wanted to commit suicide, it seemed, based on his post, that his family had turned his back on him. I knew that wasn't the message I wanted to read on social media that morning, but I couldn't change what I had already seen from the message. I closed my phone right away and shook my head from side to side, breathing heavy and trying to control my breathing. Someone said to me to open the message and respond to it. I responded to his message by telling him that God loves him and that he's not alone with whatever he was going through. I also told him that I was on my way to bury my son that morning. Right after I sent the message, I felt as though a weight was lifted off my shoulders. I didn't know this young man from anywhere, nor had I seen him in my entire life. That morning I believe I was used to send him a message that he needed to hear. I was going to ignore it at first, but I didn't feel right by just turning a blind eye. I believe that morning, that God had positioned me to do great things. I may have saved a life that day by just being the vessel used to deliver the message to the young man. As I remained seated in the car and read the message that I had sent to him over to myself, it dawned on me that the message was not just for him - it was for both of us. I didn't see the importance of me reaching out to a perfect stranger at first, but I needed the message as a reminder that morning before getting to the funeral service. I knew I needed to change my mindset, it was going to be hard, but I wanted the change as bad as I wanted air to breath. It dawned on me that my life would never be the same going forward.

As we enter the driveway and made our way walking towards the front doors again, I could hear and feel my heart beating a thousand miles per hour. Taking deep breaths, slowly pacing myself to see Noah again for the last time. I wasn't sure what to do or think at this point. I didn't have a choice as to whether I would attend the funeral. This was my son, there was no backing out, but the thought of me saying goodbye to him and thoughts that wrestled through my mind seeing him like that for the last time was unbearable. On this day, I witnessed everyone gathering and filling the room slowly. As the time went by, everyone gathered around him saying their last words. That day I lost my son Noah in the physical form and gained him in a spiritual world. I recall his sisters and close family giving speeches about him, my love letter that I wrote to him I had plans on passing it off to my aunt to read, but I couldn't do it. I wanted to talk to him and let him know how much I loved him dearly with him in my presence for the last time. As I stood up to read my love letter to Noah, my legs felt very weak, they were wobbling as I walked towards the front of the room again for the last time. As soon as I got to the front of the room and held my head up, I realized suddenly the room was full of family and friends. I didn't realize how many had filled the room that day. I realized very quickly how much love and support surrounded my family. Everyone that knew Noah or had met him was there. It was my turn to read my letter out loud, with every sentence I started, my husband would help me read and would point to some of the words. My tears sat in my eyes so heavily, it made it very hard to see the words in front of me. With my head in the clouds as I read, I could feel Noah's presence. His spirit filled the room and I could see his face smiling at each and everyone. After reading the letter and getting back to my seat, I started experiencing and feeling a spiritual connection with my son, his spirit was very strong in the room. I realized it even more when it was time for us to say our last goodbye before the closing of the casket. As I sit there and witness my family and everyone else say their last goodbyes, I felt a very eerie feeling come over me; it was a feeling of unfamiliar territories again. I was not too sure what it was, but I was open to receiving the energy that I was picking up in the room.

As the director closed the casket a feeling came over me, as though I was giving birth to Noah again; but it was a dif-ferent type of pain that I was experiencing in the spiritual sense. I could feel the contractions as they settled within my lower abdominal area, my stomach tightened more as I witnessed the casket being closed, I recall crying out. I didn't know how loud I was, but I know that there was a silence that came into the room. It lasted as though it was forever, but I knew it was only a matter of seconds. I could feel tingles through out my body from my head to my toes, and I heard nothing for what was probably about thirty seconds, but it felt as though it was much longer. It didn't dawn on me right away that I had a real connection until weeks went by after speaking to a family friend about it. I prayed about having that connection with him, searching and looking for answers that no one could give to me but God. With each prayer that I offered, God would always reveal to me the answers that I was looking for. The answers may never have been on my time but in the end, I knew I would get them eventually. I now had a new spiritual relationship with my son; others may not understand or even imagine the connection we have, but I know its real, it settled over me and gave me some sort of peace.

What I learned during this chapter:

During this chapter of my life, before I thought I have faced everything possible. When I received the news of my son it shocked every nerve in me, feeling lost broken and empty I was very angry and filled with new emotions I've never experienced before. I realize the importance of life even more and having your love ones around. When you're also faced with the worst news, surround yourself with family/friends that love and support you and someone whom will have your best interest at heart. It will be your journey and only yours, so be gentle and have patience with yourself. Trust your intuition and know that your life will never be the same. Whenever we hear that we think of the worst and it doesn't have to be the case for you. Making a spiritual connection with my son was one of the most important things, it gave me light and life and it has allowed me to speak life into anything that may seem dull or impossible.

CHAPTER FOURTEEN

Purpose driven, new relationship and a spiritual connection with Noah, overcoming obstacles that held me back.

IF I CAN share one important thing with you that stood out when my world crashed, that would be the emptiness. I wasn't just empty mentally and emotionally, I was empty physically and all the above, I felt as though I was weightless. I was walking around feeling as though I was as light as a feather, but with skeletons attached to my body. I'm sure you can imagine what that looks like, it just felt as though a hole was pierced through me walking around. I've been around many people growing up who have experienced loss, but a lot of them never explained the experience and how it impacted them. Especially growing up in a Caribbean background a lot of emotions are left unexplained or dismissed. As a young mother, it is important for me to change that for my children. I also didn't want to use my phone to speak to anyone for some reason I preferred their company, if anyone visited during the first month. One family member I really didn't want to speak to due to her negative energy, I didn't see how she could have helped me in any way then. I felt as though, with that person, it was always a one-way conversation, which didn't benefit me. During those difficult moments, I ended up not speaking to her for roughly about four months. It was not planned, but I had a conversation with myself about putting myself first before anyone else, which was hard, but I did it. Another conversation I had with myself was how was there going to be a bright side to all of this? I didn't see that it was possible at all. I was prepared to be a bitter angry and miserable person, to be honest, I wanted to be that way, but my faith did not allow that thought to consume me for too long. As much as I tried, I couldn't stay that way the world didn't need another angry person in it. I wanted to do more. As much as I was fighting with that part of me, contemplating how can I help another mother, sister, or brother who might be facing something similar? I prayed to God to use me and mold me into the vessel that he intended me to be. Little by little I started seeing the change daily in the things that I did, the places that I went and the people that I surrounded myself with. I didn't question any of it when things started unfolding. Whenever I spoke, I would try to speak positively, even on my worst days, which really helped. I was hungry for change, I wanted it as much as I wanted the air that I breathed. One of the things that took me out of my comfort zone, it was by placing myself in front of an audience of three hun-dred people and shared my experience. I wasn't nervous about any of it, it just felt right, and I will continue to speak every opportunity that's given to me. My son was always outspoken, sometimes I question myself and wonder if he is speaking through me to get his messages out? We have a spiritual connection that is very strong and many times I will ask him for directions. There are times when I will sit alone in my living room in the quiet, with no distractions of any sorts. At that point, I will take myself to an unfamiliar place. This is where I rid myself of all the grief, dark clouds and the puddles in the ground. This place is a place of tranquility and calm. I go there very often to stay focused and grounded, which will allow me to continue my journey. This is the place where I'm able to connect with Noah more. During the times that I cannot get myself to that place, my days become more challenging and it seems chaotic at times. Then I resort and think of my reason "why" and everything will always come back to my children. I do it for my kids first then for myself. They are the first thing that I think of when I am making any conscious decisions. Every day it's a journey that I am on keeping Noah's spirit alive. I know he's not here physically, but I can feel his presence and his energy. If Noah was here, I know he will speak his truth and let everyone know his story. Our relationship is different now, he gives me the drive and the energy daily to think about helping others. This is his legacy and

I'm only here to make it a reality for him. Before Noah's passing, I was asleep at some point, I believe It feels as though I fell asleep spiritually and emotionally at the age of thirteen or fourteen, but Noah has awoken me from a long sleep. I was baptised in my mid-twenties and while that was another spiritual awakening, it was different to the one I have experienced now. As much as this is hard for me to write this and say it; it feels as though Noah has given me life and made a sacrifice for me to stay awake in the spiritual sense. God and Noah are the reasons why I can wake every morning and feel as though I was given a second chance in life to make it right, right with my family and friends and with others in the world. I wake in the morning with a light lit within me that seems as though it cannot be turned off. When I heard the news of my son passing away, I thought that my life had ended for sure. I have experience enough to know what my triggers are, and for the first two months I didn't see how I was going to survive, I just went along with everything, talk about doing damage control. I went back out to work one month later. I recall being at work and during my daily routine walks, I would speak out loud to Noah, as though he was walking beside me. I would speak out loud to God as well asking Him to help me see the way and praying to Him to make a shift in my life. When I prayed, I received the answers I wanted, they didn't come crystal clear to me, but they were clear enough for me to know that changes would come, and that they were going to happen.

I was now getting visions of doing better in my life. I was going places where I've never gone and was doing things that I had never done before. I did not question it because I asked for it. My life hasn't been perfect and wasn't perfect, as you've already read in the above chapters. One of the things I prayed for and will continue pray for, is clarity and purpose; I couldn't continue to go on living without changing. I had to change my mindset and my daily habits, I felt that those were the things that were keeping me back and keeping me captive from moving forward. I've already recognized and acknowledged that this will be a lifelong journey for me, which makes it easier for me to move ahead in some respects. There were other barriers that were blocking me before in my life. Fear was number one on the list and was the biggest one of them all, I constantly lived in fear, always worried about everything and what others thought of me. I always put others first, leaving myself behind and was left with the feeling of being inadequate or not good enough. I read in another book that the acronym meaning of "F.E.A.R is Face Everything and Rise." I quickly learnt, after reading that book and faced with fear that this is what I must do. If I could face everything and rise, I would be ok going forward, I knew it will not change my circumstances, but I knew I had not much else to lose. It took years of fear, to allow me to finally overcome one of the biggest things in life that keeps a lot of us back.

I got over my fear by starting with the little things and worked my way up to the bigger ones that were affecting me and holding me back.

1. Self Sabotage - I stopped all the negative self talk

I have in my head about myself. I was always hard on myself and as much as I was preaching about being kind to yourself to my kids, I was not practicing it for myself.

2. Comfort Zone - I stepped out of my comfort zone. I made myself very uncomfortable doing things that I wasn't accustomed to; I went to events at least once a month to keep me accountable and to meet others.

3. Mindset - Changing my mindset was one of the biggest changes for me, you can say you want a change, but you must be willing to change the way you think and behave daily. It starts from within and this process will show on the outward. This was a rough process for me, I didn't make the changes over night, but I gradually stated thinking differently. This was also something that I had prayed for, as I asked God to work on me and use me as a vessel in other's lives. I had to make a change with out the self-doubt and self-sabotage.

4. Transparency – I struggled with this phase for a very long time. This stage was most challenging for me because over the years of being disappointed and let down by family and friends I've put my walls up, I've put them so high that I do not allow others into my world or open to them. I've missed many opportunities because of this. When you're transparent and seek help when needed things will

work out for you. Never be afraid or ashamed of your story or your experiences. You might be able to help others by just being who you are accepting all your imperfections.

5. Manage Fear - Do we really get over our fears? Fear will often creep up on me daily and sometimes its more difficult than at other times. I remind myself how great I am, how important I am and how much my story will help others, just one woman, one man or one child including my children in this world. I also think if I give into fear, what is the point of living? I look at fear as a thief in the night; it comes, takes whatever it wants and leaves you feeling empty and unaccomplished afterwards. Fear has also brought out the ugliest side of people and leads to unnecessary behaviour. We might feel fear before doing a presentation in front of a large crowd or doing something we know that's not in our comfort zone. However, the more we stay focused and practice using coping strategies, our efforts will eventually pay off. You will be able to go through most of your days thinking less about having any type of fear.

I noticed slowly that I was changing from within, all the things that I've doubted myself before changed about me. I noticed the changes happening from within. Sometimes I think to myself what I did to deserve Gods love for me and why is he keeping me?

I can only speak and write from my own experiences, due to my recent loss. My goal is to heal, motivate and inspire one heart at a time. Even though it causes me a lot of pain to write this book, sharing my son's life from start to finish, highlighting the highs and the lows was a very difficult process for me. There have been numerous times where I picked up my laptop and could not type a sentence. I am still in the middle of my grieving, during these times I practice and meditate while allowing myself to process what just happened. There have been several things that were crucial to the process of me piecing it all together. Ill list out the top ten that were helpful to me.

1. Allowing myself to grieve.

2. Allowing myself to cry.

3. Spend time alone to reflect.

4. Building a spiritual relationship with God and my son.

5. Speaking to my son out loud.

6. Having a close friend or family member that you can open to.

7. Journaling and writing as much as I could.

8. Networking and finding recourses that could assist me.

9. Spending time outdoors with others and taking long walks.

10. Being gentle and patient with myself.

Everything that I've outlined has helped me one hundred percent. I was desperate to find myself and to get my head out of the clouds, I sought change from the inside. There was no order or sequence to the change what I had in mind; I was active daily with ideas in my head regarding changing my pattern. Thinking about it wasn't good enough for me. I had to change from just thinking about things, to doing something. It was a scary feeling, especially if you're unsure of the outcome, but I trusted my inner voice and believed that I had the power and the ability to do anything; I committed myself to change. You might also be wondering; How I did do this with three other children? I needed to be there for them. I didn't have much of a choice when it came to that, the only thing that kept me committed and positive was I followed through on all that I've outlined above and seeing their little faces. I look at them each day and I see that they are fully dependent on me, If I fall completely apart, things will only become more difficult for them. In addition, to me being fully committed, I also think of what my son would really want if he was here. He would tell me to take care of myself and his sisters, share his story and shine my light.

Throughout it all, I kept focussed and tried to remember my reason "why?" My reason was, and has always been, my children. There's no special formula that I'm giving you. The mind is also very powerful, what you put out in the universe, is what you will get back. I try to send out good energy and speak positivity into my life. Positive affirmations have got me this far as well and are keeping me going. For example, I went to an event during the early stages of my grieving and one of my favourite Canadian authors, Makini Smith, was there promoting her book "101 Affirmations on how to get you through your healing." I didn't realize she had a book on affirmations until that day. I ended up purchasing the book at this event and its all-around affirmations printed in bold big letters, they are positive, and I practice them daily. I keep this book at the side of my bedside table, and it's a constant reminder to me of the power of positive affirmations.

Music was also my therapy, everyone will grieve differently. Don't let anyone tell you otherwise. All your days aren't going to be happy and memorable. Do not apologize for having a bad day. Take away the bad from it, learn and move ahead, working on yourself daily. Throughout my experiences I discovered that we tend to forget about ourselves a lot during two stages in our lives: having children and the loss of a child. I had the same experience twice. I recalled each time after giving birth, how much of a task it was to even find the time to do the simple things such as brushing my hair or even taking a shower. I had this same experience during the loss of my son, I was so consumed by my thoughts that they would take over my entire day and it was mentally crippling me to take care of myself. It felt as though I had become a baby again when I started hearing my aunt asking me if I had taken a shower or when she would remind me that I needed to eat. These are some of the things we take for granted and no one really explains the ugly side of things. I'm here to tell someone who might be reading this, to be gentle with yourself and take all the time you need to get to where you can see the light and feel like yourself again. A lot of people have also asked me how I'm feeling through out the process, you will get that question a lot. I simply answer them all the time expressing how I'm feeling without pretending or acting as though I have it all together, if you're having a bad day, just simply say it like it is. Just be yourself, you don't need to explain too many details for anyone.

Thank God for makeup also, especially concealer, it became my best friend through everything. I've had a lot of sleepless nights. I find that less is always baest during a difficult time.

CHAPTER FIFTEEN

LETTERS, MESSAGES AND POEMS TO NOAH

TO MY DEAR SON NOAH

I REMEMBER WHEN you were born on August 13th, 2003 at 11:08pm, 7lbs 8oz, God has blessed me with the most pre-cious gift of bringing you into my life. The moment you came into my world I knew my life would change for ever. You immediately melted my heart and gave me a reason to live forever. The smell of your skin as I pressed my nose against your soft face, your fingers were as tiny and had all the wrinkles that eventually faded away. Pure and soft, new to this world, all I wanted for you was to soar away. Wrapped up in blankets warm and snuggled I pray that you always stayed that way. As I look back on the years, I really wished you stayed. You were young, full of life, had the smarts and *the style that would always stay. Birthdays went by without a single birthday unnoticed. We celebrated life, we lived for today, for tomorrow was never promised. Your smile could light up any room. You always had me blown away with your feisty attitude and your personality. Those memories, I will always cherish and keep with me forever. Going to daycare for the first year I can still see you walk and run to me as I'm walking closer. Closer to the doorway, a doorway that changed our lives forever. Your first day of school, you acted so cool, with a smile that was worth a million dollars and you had a heart bigger than King Solomon. I remember taking the busses with you, walking to the park with you, playing on the monkey bars and swings; you would always run around until you were out of wind. Happy years, happy thoughts, happy memories I'll always cherish them all. As time went by and you got older and taller, I always told you that you were my baby and you don't know it all. You were wise, strong, caring and loved by a good family. Oh, son the memories you've given me I shall have them for eternity they will never fade if I'm living. Your sisters love and miss you daily, they will always talk about what and how you would do things daily. Your life was as precious as a little flower that just bloomed, a flower that brightens up and radiates every room. If I had the chance again, I would go back and save that precious flower; and take the place of your life that was taken away too soon. I love you my son, I love and appreciate all of you and all that God has created from the first day that you bloomed. Nights we would sit around on the couch and watch your favourite movies, you would brush my hair and sometimes rub my shoulders. Do you remember when*

I would pick you up at your father's house? Sometimes you would rush to me and other times you would pout. Full of life, with such a beautiful smile. I can still hear you calling me saying "Mama! Mama!"" as I often stare and gazed out of the window. The music that you would blast and play from your room on a weekend or sometimes during the week would always have me thinking "who is this young man that is growing up in front of my eyes? How can it be that he's so tall and full of style?" Driving for hours to and from Toronto, having to hear you and your sisters go at it, that will never fade. Those memories will always be here now and tomorrow. The years I had with you were never enough, we were just getting to know each other as the days, months and years went by. God must be pleased with you as his angel by his side, maybe one day I'll be able to sing to you a lullaby. I have so much to say to you. Do you remember in my bathroom you and your older sister acting like a fool? You were funny and full of personality, your "Madea" voice would always have us laughing, even you at time could not even keep a straight face. If only it could have lasted forever. I still sit up late at night, staring out of the window through the dark, waiting for that moonlight. I stand by your window and imagine that you'll return home; walking through the front door. I miss our times in the kitchen where you would pack away all the plastic Tupperware, wash the dishes and eat all the leftovers. As each day passes, they say time will heal, but to me I'll never be done healing. My tears flow heavily when everyone is fast asleep, praying and gazing away at your pictures that I keep next to me, whether I'm alone or in the presence of others, my mind is thinking of you, wishing and wondering when will it be my turn to see you again? I miss you and love you my son. If I could change one year, it will be your fifteenth year, I would go back and change the hands of time when you were last there. Instead of you, I wished it was me, I would have sacrificed myself, just so you could have had eternity. I will forever miss you my son, my moon and my stars. There is nothing that I wouldn't do just to have you hear my voice. Our years that we spent together, I will always hold them near in my heart, you have given me a purpose and a reason to live. When I'm doubtful of myself, I call your name as though you are right here. I've learned to cherish what we have while it's here, I've also learned that telling your story was something that I had to share. I know you must be proud of me, proud of your sisters, I pray that you are looking down from heaven.

Love always,
Mom

* FEEL ME*

Can you feel me?
You can put on your best dress
Can you feel me?
Your best pair of shoes
Can you feel me?
Paint your nails red
Can you feel me?
Wear your favourite lipstick
Can you feel me?

Laugh until your stomach hurts
Can you feel me?
Dance like there's no tomorrow
Can you feel me?
Shop at the mall where you can hardly hear your voice
Can you feel me?
You can do it all! Yes, you can
Can you feel me?
The fact remains you're still going through it all
The pain mixed with roller coaster of emotions
The thoughts everyday that always seem to linger
The emptiness that you feel like an empty vessel and the only time it's filled is when it's all flowing over
Can you feel me?

Loving Love Noah

Noah Watson:
"A name that everybody knew, even if they weren't close to him.
Noah meant so much to so many people.
He was a friend to many. An inspiration; honestly, he inspired me to take chances and never take the day for granted.
He was funny and caring and always thinking of others when things were wrong.
He was one of the funniest people I knew, and I knew I could always talk to him if I needed to smile or laugh or just feel better in general.

I trusted Noah as a person I can speak to during difficult times, he always knew how to make me feel better.
Even if someone didn't know Noah, they knew what an amazing person he was.
His personality and positivity just radiated and was felt by everyone around him.
Noah touched so many with his life and we will continue to celebrate it. He will always be with us in our hearts.
He will never be forgotten, and we love him so incredibly much."

LOVE YOU ALWAYS

Noah is in heaven with angels
We must pray for Noah
Remember you will have dreams about the good times with Noah.
He loved coming over to bring me to the park and play video games.
He loved playing basketball.
He will touch many lives and hearts and will be missed
But the class comedian will not be forgotten.

ICE COLD

Today I visited you by your grave site
It was cold and layered with ice
I cried out to you from the depth of my heart, asking you why you had to go.
Days I prayed and wished it was me, how can I have your live memory restored.

As I stood there during the dark, I wonder if my tears would stop the overflow.
Everything covered in ice I often wonder if I'll ever feel my toes.
Praying that you will come into my dreams and make this emptiness disappear, show me that it was never real and tell me you'll always be here. Your grave filled with the same blue flowers that I once laid on your stone. How could this be my view of you, when all I wanted was a lot more years.

Sing

Its been so long since I last sang you your favourite song
My rusty voice crackles as I sing the melody of the sweet rap and song
I can hear you say you cannot sing for nothing
But that's not the point, I just want to sing and make it something
A song you can hear, a song you can share, a song that will remind you of how much I care
I just want to sing
Sing loud
Sing proud
Come on and sing with me
Sing for better
Sing for joy
Sing for the love that you know will always be there

A Letter to someone Special

"Dear Mom."
"I truly thank you for everything you have done for me.
I want you to know that I pay attention to everything you do for me.
The little things and the big things
I wanted to take the time to give you recognition to many things you have done for me…
Thank you for the 9 months you carried me
The roof you put over my head
The clothes you provided
The food
The time you make for me
And your forgiveness
There are so many things you have done for me, it gets hard to even keep track of it all.
All the fun, laughter, games, jokes, miss understandings those are all the things that make us a family
The greatest gift you have given me is being your son and for that I truly thank you!"

From Noah Watson
Dec.6th, 2016

A Lullaby

Your soft voice saying goodnight
A memory that will last forever
A story that will change hearts all together
It still feels like a deep sleep
I'm trying to wake up from having that terrible dream

Everyone is sound asleep; I'm still waiting for you maybe ill hear your keys.
Walking up and down the halls, I tell myself you're sound asleep
Did you hear my lullaby?
Did you fall into a dream with me by your side?
Singing
Singing something that you like, you choose your own melody.
If it's sweet, I hope it brings you back good memories.
As I rock you good night
I can hear your heartbeat
That's my baby's lullaby memory

A Prayer for Noah

Dear God, thank you for blessing me with my beautiful son Noah, thank you for bringing him into my life. He has made me into the person that I am today. Thank you for always guiding and protecting him throughout his life, I pray that you will continue to mold him in heaven and show up for him in his time of need. I pray that you will cleanse him and renew his spirit. I lift him up to you Lord as your son, as my guiding angel now from heaven. Cover him under your wings daily as he rests in eternal peace.
I pray for his soul to be at rest.
I pray for love to surround him
I pray for peace
I pray for his forgiveness in anything he's done wrong
I pray for a good spirit

I pray for calm
I pray for light
I pray for his sisters and brothers to meet with him again
I pray to reunite and be one again with him
I pray for his heart to be at ease
I pray for his eternal blessings in your kingdom and for all the angels to surround him showing him love, joy, peace and favour.

FINAL THOUGHTS

To my beautiful children who are still here with me in the flesh Taijah, Brianna, and Christina, I pray that you are inspired from reading this book and may it always be a constant reminder to you that you are loved, you are beautiful and you are enough. Without each of you I will not be the person I am today. You will always be my reason why. I also pray that wherever life may take you, you'll find peace and comfort in this book. Honouring your brother this way was my wish for his 16th birthday. As you turn each chapter remember that all things are possible no matter the odds or what may come your way. You are powerful and every question that you have, the answers will always be inside of you. To my Aunt Luenda Bib-by, thank you for always being my rock and one of my biggest supporters over the years, thank you for always believ-ing in me. To my brothers and sisters Thank you for always being you, without you I will not be who I am today. To my husband thank you for you support and love you've displayed along the way, without you and your family I will not be the mother I am today. For each and everyone who have read this book I pray that whatever it is you're experiencing in life you're able to take positive action steps into the right direction, use this book as somewhat of a guide or tool to help you level up into the next dimension of your life. For every mother out there, who have experienced loss you are not alone, I send peace and love to you wherever you are in the entire universe.

Join me
Facebook-I.S.H I'm Still Healing
Instagram-fifteenyears14chapters
Website-www.nataliewatson.me

www.ingramcontent.com/pod-product-compliance
Lightning Source LLC
Chambersburg PA
CBHW020533080526
44583CB00013B/851